ISBN 978-0-365-23981-9
PIBN 11265369

WATER SUPPLY OUTLOOK FOR WASHINGTON

U. S. DEPARTMENT of AGRICULTURE ★ SOIL CONSERVATION SERVICE

Collaborating with

DEPARTMENT OF ECOLOGY STATE OF WASHINGTON

Data included in this report were obtained by the agencies named above in cooperation with Federal, State and private organizations listed inside the back cover of this report.

AS OF
MAR. 1, 1977

TO RECIPIENTS OF WATER SUPPLY OUTLOOK REPORTS:

Most of the usable water in western states originates as mountain snowfall. This snowfall accumulates during the winter and spring, several months before the snow melts and appears as streamflow. Since the runoff from precipitation as snow is delayed, estimates of snowmelt runoff can be made well in advance of its occurrence. Streamflow forecasts published in this report are based principally on measurement of the water equivalent of the mountain snowpack.

Forecasts become more accurate as more of the data affecting runoff are measured. All forecasts assume that climatic factors during the remainder of the snow accumulation and melt season will interact with a resultant average effect on runoff. Early season forecasts are therefore subject to a greater change than those made on later dates.

The snow course measurement is obtained by sampling snow depth and water equivalent at surveyed and marked locations in mountain areas. A total of about ten samples are taken at each location. The average of these are reported as snow depth and water equivalent. These measurements are repeated in the same location near the same dates each year.

Snow surveys are made monthly or semi-monthly from January 1 through June 1 in most states. There are about 1900 snow courses in Western United States and in the Columbia Basin in British Columbia. Networks of automatic snow water equivalent and related data sensing devices, along with radio telemetry are expanding and will provide a continuous record of snow water and other parameters at key locations.

Detailed data on snow course and soil moisture measurements are presented in state and local reports. Other data on reservoir storage, summaries of precipitation, current streamflow, and soil moisture conditions at valley elevations are also included. The report for Western United States presents a broad picture of water supply outlook conditions, including selected streamflow forecasts, summary of snow accumulation to date, and storage in larger reservoirs.

Snow survey and soil moisture data for the period of record are published by the Soil Conservation Service by states about every five years. Data for the current year is summarized in a West-wide basic data summary and published about October 1 of each year.

COVER PHOTO: SNOW COURSE MEASUREMENTS BY A SURVEY TEAM IN UTAH'S WASATCH RANGE.
ORC-254-10

PUBLISHED BY SOIL CONSERVATION SERVICE

The Soil Conservation Service publishes reports following the principal snow survey dates from January 1 through June 1 in cooperation with state water administrators, agricultural experiment stations and others. Copies of the reports for Western United States and all state reports may be obtained from Soil Conservation Service, West Technical Service Center, Room 510, 511 N.W. Broadway, Portland, Oregon 97209.

Copies of state and local reports may also be obtained from state offices of the Soil Conservation Service in the following states:

STATE	ADDRESS
Alaska	Room 129, 2221 East Northern Lights Blvd., Anchorage, Alaska 99504
Arizona	Room 3008, 6029 Federal Building, Phoenix, Arizona 85025
Colorado (N. Mex.)	P. O. Box 17107, Denver, Colorado 80217
Idaho	Room 345, 304 N. 8th. St., Boise, Idaho 83702
Montana	P.O. Box 98, Bozeman, Montana 59715
Nevada	P. O. Box 4850, Reno Nevada 89505
Oregon	1220 S.W. Third Ave., Portland, Oregon 97204
Utah	4012 Federal Bldg., 125 South State St., Salt Lake City, Utah 84138
Washington	360 U.S. Court House, Spokane, Washington 99201
Wyoming	P. O. Box 2440, Casper, Wyoming 82602

PUBLISHED BY OTHER AGENCIES

Water Supply Outlook reports prepared by other agencies include a report for California by the Water Supply Forecast and Snow Surveys Unit, California Department of Water Resources, P. O. Box 388, Sacramento, California 95802 --- and for British Columbia by the Department of Lands, Forests and Water Resources, Water Resources Service, Parliament Building, Victoria, British Columbia

U.S. DEPARTMENT of AGRICULTURE SOIL CONSERVATION SERVICE
CONSERVATION OF WATER BEGINS WITH THE SNOW SURVEY

USDA SCS-PORTLAND OR 1976

WATER SUPPLY OUTLOOK
FOR
WASHINGTON

and
FEDERAL - STATE - PRIVATE COOPERATIVE SNOW SURVEYS

Issued by

R.M. DAVIS
ADMINISTRATOR
SOIL CONSERVATION SERVICE
WASHINGTON, D C

Released by

GALEN S. BRIDGE
STATE CONSERVATIONIST
SOIL CONSERVATION SERVICE
SPOKANE, WASHINGTON

In Cooperation with

WILBUR G. HALLAUER
DIRECTOR
DEPARTMENT OF ECOLOGY
STATE OF WASHINGTON

Report prepared by

ROBERT T. DAVIS, Snow Survey Supervisor
and
NORINE P. KENT, Statistical Assistant

SOIL CONSERVATION SERVICE
360 U.S. COURTHOUSE
SPOKANE, WASHINGTON 99201

NING

You may have less Irrigation water this year than ever before.

SNOW COURSE MEASUREMENTS MADE ON MARCH 1, 1977 CONTINUE TO INDICATE THAT MANY AREAS WILL HAVE SEVERE TO CRITICAL WATER SHORTAGES. STUDY THE ATTACHED WATER SUPPLY FORECAST CAREFULLY FOR STREAM FLOW AND/OR RESERVOIR STORAGE FIGURES THAT CONCERN YOUR AREA. KEEP IN TOUCH WITH YOUR IRRIGATION DISTRICT OR OTHER OFFICIALS FOR ESTIMATES OF THE SUPPLY AVAILABLE FOR YOU. YOU MAY FIND YOU'LL NEED TO CHANGE CROPS, PLANTED ACREAGE, TIMING OF WATER APPLICATION OR EFFICIENCY OF YOUR WATER DISTRIBUTION SYSTEM. THESE ARE SOME OF THE EARLY DECISIONS AND PLANS YOU MAY HAVE TO MAKE:

1. Change to crops which require less water.

2. Reduce the crop acreage. Naturally, this will affect the fertilizer you order and the amount of seed you buy. Be sure unplanted land has cover crops to prevent wind erosion.

3. Check out your irrigation systems carefully. Make certain that ditches have no water-wasting weeds or debris to slow delivery; that sprinkler heads don't have leaks, pipes have tight connections and pumps work properly. If new parts or equipment are needed, purchase them soon.

4. Plant only the best land - it makes most efficient use of water. If your soil has been mapped, local Soil Conservation Service personnel can guide you. If not mapped, they can still give you general information.

5. Maintain close contact with the Soil Conservation Service or your local Conservation District for the latest water supply forecasts, and for soil information. SCS has just published water conservation TIPS pamphlets for irrigators, farmers and ranchers. Get copies.

6. Maintain close contact with the Agricultural Stabilization and Conservation Service county office. Funds for cost sharing on special water stretching practices may be made available because of the drought situation. ASCS also administers the Federal Disaster Assistance program.

7. Do the same with your closest Farmers Home Administration office. Special loans may become available.

8. Do the same with the local Cooperative Extension Service office for current information on crops, feed supply and marketing.

SCS, ASCS AND FMHA ARE LISTED IN THE PHONE BOOK UNDER "U.S. GOVERNMENT, AGRICULTURE, DEPARTMENT OF." THE EXTENSION SERVICE IS USUALLY LISTED WITH LOCAL COUNTY OFFICES.

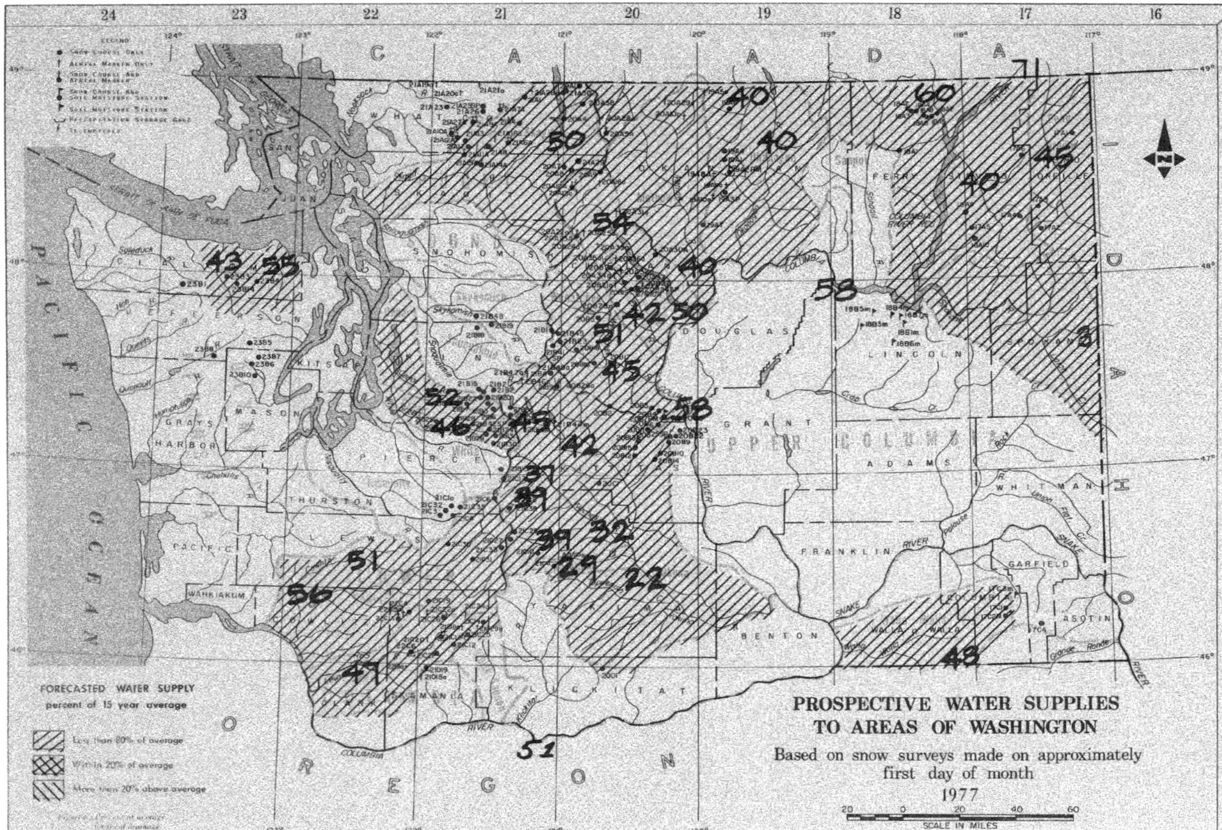
PROSPECTIVE WATER SUPPLIES
TO AREAS OF WASHINGTON
Based on snow surveys made on approximately
first day of month
1977
SCALE IN MILES
20 0 20 40 60
FORECASTED WATER SUPPLY
percent of 15 year average
Less than 80% of average
Within 20% of average
More than 20% above average
CANADA
IDAHO
OREGON
PACIFIC OCEAN
COLUMBIA
RIVER
SNAKE
DOUGLAS
LINCOLN
GRANT
ADAMS
FRANKLIN
BENTON
WHITMAN
GARFIELD
ASOTIN
WALLA WALLA
KLICKITAT
SKAMANIA
CLARK
COWLITZ
WAHKIAKUM
PACIFIC
THURSTON
PIERCE
MASON
GRAYS HARBOR
JEFFERSON
CLALLAM
KITSAP
SNOHOMISH
FERRY
SPOKANE
UPPER COLUMBIA
24 23 22 21 20 19 18 17 16
A B C D

INDEX to WASHINGTON SNOW COURSES, SOIL MOISTURE STATIONS and PRECIPITATION STORAGE GAGES

UPPER [illegible]A DRAINAGE

NAME	NUMBER	SEC.	TWP.	RANGE	ELEV.
Pend Oreille River					
Boyen Mountain	17A2	7	31N	43E	5250
Bunchgrass Meadow	17A1	24	37N	44E	5000
Winchester Creek	17A3	30	33N	43E	2970
Kettle River					
Boulder Road	18A2	36	39N	36E	1450
Butte Creek	18A3	28	39N	35E	4070
Cabin Creek	18A8	5	38N	36E	3170
Goat Creek	18A1	26	39N	35E	3595
Snow Caps Creek	18A5	3	38N	36E	2150
Snow Caps Trail	18A6	5	38N	36E	2720
Summit G S	18A7	20	39N	35E	4600
Colville River					
Baird	17A6	19	36N	42E	3215
Carlson	18A9	34	32N	38E	2885
Chewelah	17A4	11	32N	41E	4925
Stranger Mountain	17A5	26	31N	38E	4990
Togo	18A10	6	29N	38E	3370
Sanpoil River					
Sherman Creek Pass	18A1	19	36N	35E	5350
Okanogan River					
Clark	19A8a	2	36N	23E	7000
Muckamuck	19A9a	20	36N	24E	6750
Mutton Creek No. 1	19A1	30	37N	24E	5700
Mutton C eek No 2	19A4	19	37N	24E	6000
Paysayten	20A28a	32	40N	18E	4300
Rusty C ek	19A3P	18	35N	24E	4000
Salmon Meadows	19A2PM	33	37N	24E	4500
Starvation Mtn	19A10a	15	35N	23E	6750
Touts Coulee	19A6	30	39N	25E	2845
Methow River					
Billy Goat Pass	20A10a	10	38N	20E	6400
Dollar Watch	20A29a	8	39N	20E	7000
Harts Pass	20A5A	7	37N	18E	6500
Horseshoe Basin	19A5a	15	40N	23E	7000
Loup Loup	19A7	36	34N	23E	4650
Chelan [illegible]e Basin					
Cloudy Pass	20A22a	12	31N	15E	6500
Greenwood Flat	20A25a	3	31N	16E	3540
Little Meadows	20A24a	8	31N	16E	5275
Lyman Lake	20A23a	18	31N	16E	5900
Park Creek Flat	20A13a	19	34N	16E	2220
Park Creek Ridge	20A12A	18	34N	16E	4600
Petersons	20A16a	3	34N	17E	3730
Rainy Pass	20A9	21	35N	17E	4780
Safety Harbor	20A30A	32	31N	20E	6300
War Creek Pass	20A31a	34	33N	18E	6500
Entiat River					
Blue Creek G.S.	20B28a	19	28N	18E	5425
Brief	20B19	34	28N	19E	1600
Entiat Meadows	20A33a	28	31N	17E	4540
Entiat River Trail	20A34a	2	29N	17E	3325
Four Mile Ridge	20B27a	15	28N	19E	6800
Fox Camp	20A36a	17	30N	18E	6510
Pope Ridge	20B20	22	29N	18E	3540
Pope Ridge Snow Pillow	20B24SP	22	29N	18E	3540
Pugh Ridge	20A32a	34	30N	18E	6725
Shady Pass	20A37	20	29N	19E	6200
Snow Brushy	20A35a	21	30N	17E	3910
Tommy Creek	20B21a	10	28N	18E	4900
Wenatchee River					
Berne-Mill Creek	21B23	7	26N	15E	3170
Berne-Mill Creek (New)	21B41SP	13	26N	14E	3240
Blewett Pass No 2	20B2	35	22N	17E	4270
Chiwaukum G S	20B16	4	25N	17E	1810
Lake Wenatchee	20B5	33	27N	17E	1970
Leavenworth R S	20B17	1	24N	17E	1127
Merritt	20B18	4	26N	16E	2140
Stevens Pass	21B1	14	26N	13E	4070
Stevens Pass Sand Shed	21B45	12	26N	19E	3700
Wenatchee Ri er (continued)					
Trough #2	20B25SP	10	20N	20E	5310
Colockum Creek					
Colockum Creek Upper	20B22	11	20N	20E	5300
Colockum C eek Lower	20B23	1	20N	20E	4300
Squilchuck Creek					
Beehive Springs	20B3	12	21N	19E	4400
Scout-A-Vista	20B4	18	21N	20E	3400
Stemilt Creek					
Jump-Off	20B8	34	21N	20E	4450
Stemilt Slide	20B6	30	21N	20E	5000
Uppen Wheeler	20B7PM	30	21N	20E	4400
Crab Creek					
Creston-Kunz	18B1m	32	27N	34E	2440
Jack Woods	18B3m	28	27N	31E	2750
Krause	18B4m	21	27N	33E	2420
Sheffels	18B5m	17	27N	32E	2378
Sherman	18B7m	24	27N	33E	2440
Wheatridge	18B6m	24	25N	32E	2290
Yakima River					
Ahtanum R S	21C11	24	12N	14E	3100
Big Boulder Creek	21B9	35	23N	14E	3200
Bumping Lake	21C8	23	16N	12E	3450
Bumping Lake New	21C36	13	16N	12E	3400
Bumping Ridge	21C38P	9	15N	12E	4600
Colockum Pass	20B9	25	20N	20E	5370
Cooke Creek	20B10	17	19N	20E	4123
Domery Flat	21B44m	15	20N	14E	2200
Fish Lake	21B4	28	24N	14E	3371
Green Lake	21C10	3	12N	13E	6000
Grouse Camp	20B11	29	21N	19E	5385
High Creek	20B12	34	20N	19E	2930
Joe Lake	21B46a	22	23N	12E	4624
Lake Cle Elum	21B14M	15	20N	14E	2200
Lemah Creek	21B47a	7	23N	13E	3327
Manastash	20C1	24	17N	16E	3935
Morse Lake	21C17	6	16N	11E	5400
Nanum	20B13	4	20N	19E	3875
Trail C eek	20B14	20	19N	20E	3360
Tunnel Avenue	21B8	13	21N	11E	2450
Van Epps Pass	20B26a	16	23N	15E	5925
Walters Flat	20B15	22	20N	19E	3360
Waptus Lake	21B49a	12	23N	13E	3024
White Pass (East Side)	21C28	2	13N	11E	4500
White Pass (Leach Lake)	21C27	1	13N	11E	4500

LOWER COLUMBIA DRAINAGE

NAME	NUMBER	SEC.	TWP.	RANGE	ELEV.
Asotin Creek					
Spruce Springs	17C4	9	8N	40E	5700
Mill Creek					
Couse	17C3m	2	9N	40E	3370
Homestead	17C1	11	9N	40E	4030
Martin Springs (Helmers SM)	17C2M	23	9N	40E	4400
Klickitat River					
Satus Pass	20D1	21	6N	17E	4030
White Salmon River					
Cultus Creek	21C12	35	7N	8E	4000
Lewis River					
Blue Lake	21C22a	19	9N	8E	4800
Bob's Trail	21C21	25	8N	7E	2200
Calamity Ridge	22D1a	8	5N	5E	2500
Council Pass	21C18a	24	9N	9E	4200
Lewis River (continued)					
Divide Meadow	21C29a	21	9N	10E	5600
Grand Meadow	21C25	28	8N	9E	3500
Lone Pine Shelter	21C26	8	9N	7E	3800
Marble Mountain	22C5a	24	8N	5E	3200
New Muddy River	22C6	36	8N	6E	2000
Oldman Pass	21D19	22	6N	7E	3100
Plains of Abraham	22C1a	35	9N	5E	4400
Smith Creek Road	22C4	29	9N	6E	2100
Spencer Meadow	21C20a	16	8N	7E	3400
Surprise Lakes	21C13A	14	7N	8E	4250
Table Mountain	21C24a	20	9N	9E	4200
Timbered Peak	21D18a	36	6N	6E	3000
Cowlitz River					
Cayuse Pass	21C6	15	16N	10E	5300
Mosquito Meadows	21C19	33	10N	7E	4100
Ohanapecosh	21C32	28	15N	10E	2200
Packwood Lake	21C31	21	13N	10E	2870
Pigtail Peak	21C33	11	13N	11E	5900
Potato Hill	21C14	36	10N	10E	4500
Willame Creek	21C30	3	13N	8E	3250

PUGET SOUND DRAINAGE

NAME	NUMBER	SEC.	TWP.	RANGE	ELEV.
Nisqually River					
Ghost Forest	21C4	23	15N	8E	4550
Longmire	21C3	29	15N	8E	2760
Paradise Park (New)	21C35	13	15N	8E	5500
Stem Glade	21C1	13	15N	8E	5050
[illegible]te River					
Corral Pass	21B13	30	18N	11E	6000
Green River					
Airstrip	21B24	18	20N	11E	1800
Charley Creek	21B25	27	21N	8E	1200
Cougar Mountain	21B42SP	21	21N	9E	3200
Grass Mountain No. 2	21B27	14	20N	8E	2900
Grass Mountain No 3	21B28	12	20N	8E	2100
Lester Creek	21B29	36	20N	10E	3100
Lynn Lake	21B50	22	20N	8E	4000
Sawmill Ridge	21B31	5	19N	11E	4700
Snowshoe Butte	21B43SP	14	20N	11E	5000
Stampede Pass	21B10	25	21N	11E	3860
Twin [illegible]p	21B30	18	19N	11E	4100
Cedar River					
City Cabin	21B3	10	21N	10E	2390
Mt Gardner	21B21	33	22N	10E	3300
Mt Gardner Aux	21B22	31	22N	10E	2500
Mt. Lindsay	21B16	31	22N	9E	2500
Mt. Washington	21B15	8	22N	9E	3000
Rex River	21B17	11	21N	9E	2400
South Fork Cedar	21B6	24	21N	10E	3000
Tinkham Creek	21B20	1	21N	10E	3400
Snoqualmie River					
Alpine Meadow	21B48	31	27N	9E	3500
Olallie Meadows	21B2	19	22N	11E	3625
South Fork Tolt	21B18	26	26N	9E	1900
Skykomish River					
Lake Elizabeth	21B19	33	26N	10E	2900
Skagit River					
Beaver Creek Trail	21A4	35	39N	12E	2200
Beaver Pass	21A1	9	39N	12E	3680
Brown Top	21A28a	26	40N	12E	6000
Devils Park	20A4	34	38N	16E	5900
Freezeout Creek Trail	20A1	14	40N	14E	3500
Freezeout Meadows New	20A38	8	40N	16E	5000
Granite Creek	21A29	25	36N	16E	3500
Meadows Cabins	20A8	29	36N	14E	1900
New Hozomeen Lake	20A7	19	40N	14E	2800
Thunder Basin	21A30	10	35N	14E	4200
Baker River					
Baker Pass	21A27a	1	37N	7E	4900
Dock Butte	21A11A	8	36N	8E	3800
Easy Pass	21A7A	19	39N	11E	5200
Jasper Pass	21A6A	17	38N	11E	5400
Komo Kulshan	21A17	31	37N	9E	800
Marten Lake	21A9A	23	38N	8E	3600
Mount Blum	21A18a	27	38N	10E	5800
Rocky Creek	21A12A	20	37N	8E	2100
Schreibers Meadow	21A10A	18	37N	8E	3400
S F Thunder Creek	21A14A	20	36N	9E	2200
Sulphur Creek	21A13	22	37N	8E	1600
Three Mile Creek	21A15	18	36N	9E	1600
Watson Lakes	21A8	25	37N	9E	4500
Nooksack River					
Bald Mountain	21A19a	7	40N	7E	4400
Canyon	21A20A	20	40N	8E	5100
Glacier Creek	21A23	9-10	38N	7E	3700
Panorama New	21A26	17	39N	9E	4300
Panorama Snow Pillow	21A25SP	17	39N	9E	4300
Twin Lakes	21A21a	16	40N	9E	5200

OLYMPIC PENINSULA

NAME	NUMBER	SEC.	TWP.	RANGE	ELEV.
Dungeness River					
Deer Park	23B4	1	28N	5W	5200
Morse Creek					
Cox Valley	23B14	31	29N	6W	4500
Elwha River					
Hurricane	23B3	36	29N	7W	4500
Skokomish River					
Black and White	23B7	17	24N	5W	4200
Black and White Lakes	23B6	16	24N	5W	4700
Four Stream	23B10	1	23N	6W	3000
Home Sweet Home	23B5	28	25N	5W	5200
Sundown Pass	23B8	25	24N	7W	3900
Soleduck River					
Deer Lake	23B1	14	28N	9W	3900

LEGEND

NUMBERING SYSTEM EXAMPLE

21A7	Snow Course Only
21A7a	Aerial Marker Only
21A7A	Snow Course and Aerial Marker
21A7M	Snow Course and Soil Moisture Station
21A7m	Soil Moisture Station
21A7P	Snow Course and Precipitation Storage Gage
21A7p	Precipitation Storage Gage
21A7SP	Snow Pillow

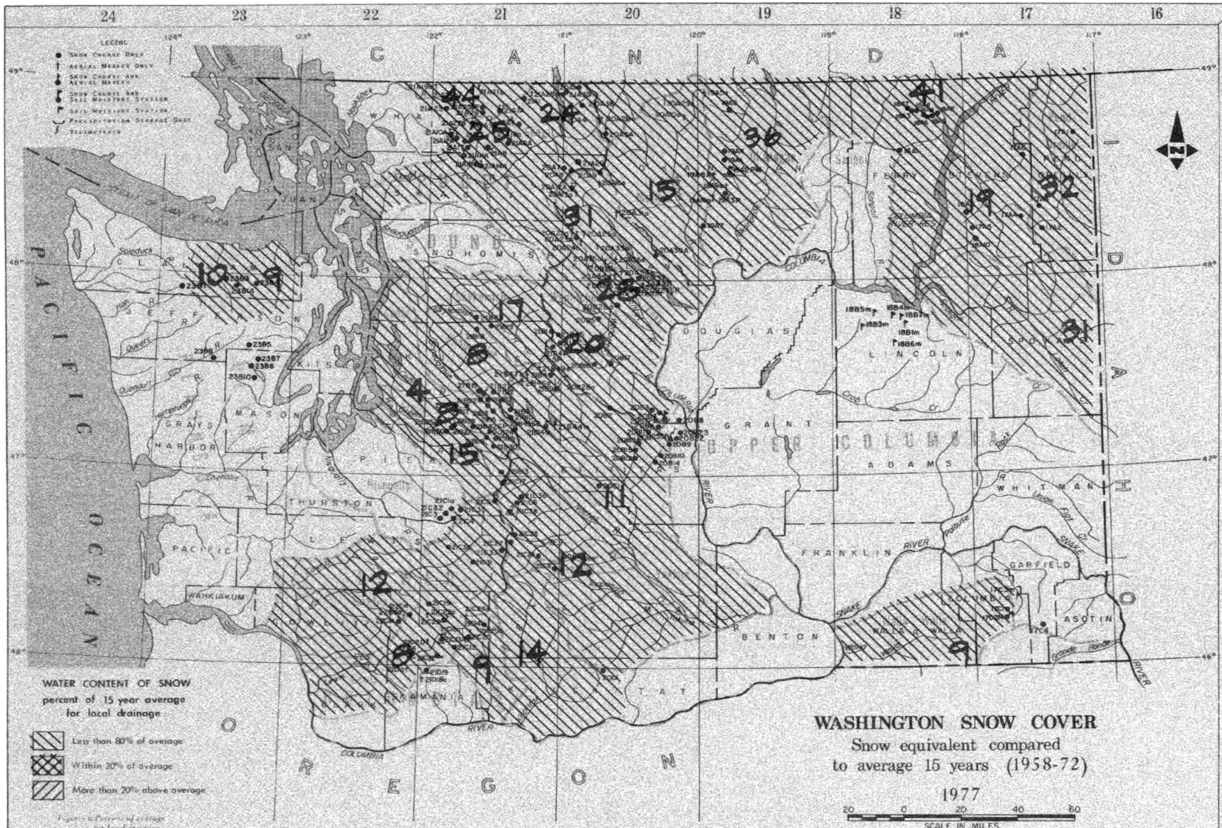
WASHINGTON SNOW COVER
Snow equivalent compared
to average 15 years (1958-72)
1977
SCALE IN MILES
WATER CONTENT OF SNOW
percent of 15 year average
for local drainage
Less than 80% of average
Within 20% of average
More than 20% above average
PACIFIC OCEAN
CANADA
IDAHO
OREGON
JEFFERSON
MASON
GRAYS HARBOR
THURSTON
PACIFIC
WAHKIAKUM
SNOHOMISH
DOUGLAS
GRANT
LINCOLN
ADAMS
FRANKLIN
BENTON
WHITMAN
GARFIELD
ASOTIN
WALLA WALLA
FERRY
STEVENS
SPOKANE
COLUMBIA
RIVER
SNAKE

INDEX to WASHINGTON SNOW COURSES, SOIL MOISTURE STATIONS and PRECIPITATION STORAGE GAGES

NAME	NUMBER	SEC.	TWP.	RANGE	ELEV.
UPPER COLUMBIA DRAINAGE					
Pend Oreille River					
Boyen Mountain	17A2	7	31N	43E	5250
Bunchgrass Meadow	17A1	24	37N	44E	5000
Winchester Creek	17A3	30	33N	43E	2970
Kettle River					
Boulder Road	18A2	36	39N	36E	1450
Butte Creek	18A3	28	39N	35E	4070
Cabin Creek	18A8	5	38N	36E	3170
Goat Creek	18A4	26	39N	35E	3595
Snow Caps C eek	18A5	3	38N	36E	2150
Snow Caps Trail	18A6	5	38N	36E	2720
Summit G S	18A7	20	39N	35E	4600
Colville River					
Baird	17A6	19	36N	42E	3215
Carlson	18A9	34	32N	38E	2885
Chewelah	17A4	11	32N	41E	4925
Stranger Mountain	17A5	26	31N	38E	4990
Togo	18A10	6	29N	38E	3370
Sanpoil River					
Sherman Creek Pass	18A1	19	36N	35E	5350
Okanogan River					
Clark	19A8a	2	36N	23E	7000
Muckamuck	19A9a	20	36N	24E	6750
Mutton C eek No 1	19A1	30	37N	24E	5700
Mutton C eek No 2	19A4	19	37N	24E	6000
Paysayten	20A28a	32	40N	18E	4300
Rusty Creek	19A3P	18	35N	24E	4000
Salmon Meadows	19A2PM	33	37N	24E	4500
Starvation Mtn	19A10a	15	35N	23E	6750
Touts Coulee	19A6	30	39N	25E	2845
Methow River					
Billy Goat Pass	20A10a	10	38N	20E	6400
Dollar Watch	20A29a	8	39N	20E	7000
Harts Pass	20A5A	7	37N	18E	6500
Horseshoe Basin	19A5a	15	40N	23E	7000
Loup Loup	19A7	36	34N	23E	4650
Chelan Lake Basin					
Cloudy Pass	20A22a	12	31N	15E	6500
Greenwood Flat	20A25a	3	31N	16E	3540
Little Meadows	20A24a	8	31N	16E	5275
Lyman Lake	20A23a	18	31N	16E	5900
Park Creek Flat	20A13a	19	34N	16E	2220
Park Creek Ridge	20A12A	18	34N	16E	4600
Petersons	20A16a	3	34N	17E	3730
Rainy Pass	20A9	21	35N	17E	4780
Safety Harbor	20A30A	32	31N	20E	6300
War Creek Pass	20A31a	34	33N	18E	6500
Entiat River					
Blue Creek G S	20B28a	19	28N	18E	5425
Brief	20B19	34	28N	19E	1600
Entiat Meadows	20A33a	28	31N	17E	4540
Enti n River Trail	20A34a	2	29N	17E	3325
Four Mile Ridge	20B27a	15	28N	19E	6800
Fox Camp	20A36a	17	30N	18E	6510
Pope Ridge	20B20	22	29N	18E	3540
Pope Ridge Snow Pillow	20B24SP	22	29N	18E	3540
Pugh Ridge	20A32a	34	30N	18E	6725
Shady Pass	20A37	20	29N	19E	6200
Snow Brushy	20A35a	21	30N	17E	3910
Tommy Creek	20B21a	10	28N	18E	4900
Wenatchee River					
Berne-Mill C eek	21B23	7	26N	15E	3170
Berne-Mill Creek (New)	21B41SP	13	26N	14E	3240
Blewett Pass No 2	20B2	35	22N	17E	4270
[illegible]kum G S	20B16	4	25N	17E	1810
Lake Wenatchee	20B5	33	27N	17E	1970
Leavenworth R S	20B17	1	24N	17E	1127
Merritt	20B18	4	26N	16E	2140
Stevens Pass	21B1	14	26N	13E	4070
Stevens Pass Sand Shed	21B45	12	26N	19E	3700

NAME	NUMBER	SEC.	TWP.	RANGE	ELEV.
Wenatchee River (continued)					
Trough #2	20B25SP	10	20N	20E	5310
Colockum Creek					
Colockum Creek Upper	20B22	11	20N	20E	5300
Colockum Creek Lower	20B23	1	20N	20E	4300
Squilchuck Creek					
Beehive Springs	20B3	12	21N	19E	4400
Scout-A-Vista	20B4	18	21N	20E	3400
Stemilt Creek					
Jump-Off	20B8	34	21N	20E	4450
Stemilt Slide	20B6	30	21N	20E	5000
Upper Wheeler	20B7PM	30	21N	20E	4400
Crab Creek					
Creston-Kunz	18B1m	32	27N	34E	2440
Jack Woods	18B3m	28	27N	31E	2750
Krause	18B4m	21	27N	33E	2420
Sheffels	18B5m	17	27N	32E	2378
Sherman	18B7m	24	27N	33E	2440
Wheatridge	18B6m	24	25N	32E	2290
Yakima River					
Ahtanum R S.	21C11	24	12N	14E	3100
Big Boulder Creek	21B9	35	25N	14E	3200
Bumping Lake	21C8	23	16N	12E	3450
Bumping Lake New	21C36	13	16N	12E	3400
Bumping Ridge	21C38P	9	15N	12E	4600
Colockum Pass	20B9	25	20N	20E	5370
Cooke Creek	20B10	17	19N	20E	4123
Domery Flat	21B44m	15	20N	14E	2200
Fish Lake	21B4	28	24N	14E	3371
Green Lake	21C10	3	12N	13E	6000
Grouse Camp	20B11	29	21N	19E	5385
High Creek	20B12	34	20N	19E	2930
Joe Lake	21B46m	22	23N	12E	4624
Lake Cle Elum	21B14M	15	20N	14E	2200
Lemah Creek	21B47m	7	23N	13E	3327
Manastash	20C1	24	17N	16E	3935
Morse Lake	21C17	6	16N	11E	5400
Nanum	20B13	4	20N	19E	3875
Trail Creek	20B14	20	19N	20E	3360
Tunnel Avenue	21B8	13	21N	11E	2450
Van Epps Pass	20B26a	16	23N	15E	5925
Walters Flat	20B15	22	20N	19E	3360
Waptus Lake	21B49a	12	23N	13E	3024
White Pass (East Side)	21C28	2	13N	11E	4500
White Pass (Leach Lake)	21C27	1	13N	11E	4500
LOWER COLUMBIA DRAINAGE					
Asotin Creek					
Spruce Springs	17C4	9	8N	40E	5700
Mill Creek					
Couse	17C3m	2	9N	40E	3370
Homestead	17C1	11	9N	40E	4030
Martin Springs (Helmers SM)	17C2M	23	9N	40E	4400
Klickitat River					
Satus Pass	20D1	21	6N	17E	4030
White Salmon River					
Cultus Creek	21C12	35	7N	8E	4000
Lewis River					
Blue Lake	21C22a	19	9N	8E	4800
Bob's Trail	21C21	25	8N	7E	2200
Calamity Ridge	22D1a	8	5N	5E	2500
Council Pass	21C18a	24	9N	9E	4200

NAME	NUMBER	SEC.	TWP.	RANGE	ELEV.
Lewis River (continued)					
Divide Meadow	21C29a	21	9N	10E	5600
Grand Meadow	21C25	28	8N	9E	3500
Lone Pine Shelter	21C26	8	9N	7E	3800
Marble Mountain	22C5a	24	8N	5E	3200
New Muddy River	22C6	36	8N	6E	2000
Oldman Pass	21D19	22	6N	7E	3100
Plains of Abraham	22C1a	35	9N	5E	4400
Smith Creek Road	22C4	29	9N	6E	2100
Spencer Meadow	21C20a	16	8N	7E	3400
Surprise Lakes	21C13A	14	7N	8E	4250
Table Mountain	21C24a	20	9N	9E	4200
Timbered Peak	21D18a	36	6N	6E	3000
Cowlitz River					
Cayuse Pass	21C6	15	16N	10E	5300
Mosquito Meadows	21C19	33	10N	7E	4100
Ohanapecosh	21C32	28	15N	10E	2200
Packwood Lake	21C31	21	13N	10E	2870
Pigtail Peak	21C33	11	13N	11E	5900
Potato Hill	21C14	36	10N	10E	4500
Willame Creek	21C30	3	13N	8E	3250
PUGET SOUND DRAINAGE					
Nisqually River					
Ghost Forest	21C4	23	15N	8E	4550
Longmire	21C3	29	15N	8E	2760
Paradise Park (New)	21C35	13	15N	8E	5500
Stem Glade	21C1	13	15N	8E	5050
White River					
Corral Pass	21B13	30	18N	11E	6000
Green River					
Airstrip	21B24	18	20N	11E	1800
Charley Creek	21B25	27	21N	8E	1200
Cougar Mountain	21B42SP	21	21N	9E	3200
Grass Mountain No. 2	21B27	14	20N	8E	2900
Grass Mountain No. 3	21B28	12	20N	8E	2100
Lester Creek	21B29	36	20N	10E	3100
Lynn Lake	21B50	22	20N	8E	4000
Sawmill Ridge	21B31	5	19N	11E	4700
Snowshoe Butte	21B43SP	14	20N	11E	5000
Stampede Pass	21B10	25	21N	11E	3860
Twin Camp	21B30	18	19N	11E	4100
Cedar River					
City Cabin	21B3	10	21N	10E	2390
Mt Gardner	21B21	30	22N	10E	3300
Mt. Gardner Aux.	21B22	31	22N	10E	2500
Mt. Lindsay	21B16	31	22N	9E	2500
Mt. Washington	21B15	8	22N	9E	3000
Rex River	21B17	11	21N	9E	2400
South Fork Cedar	21B6	24	21N	10E	3000
Tinkham Creek	21B20	1	21N	10E	3400
Snoqualmie River					
Alpine Meadow	21B48	31	27N	9E	3500
Olallie Meadows	21B2	19	22N	11E	3625
South Fork Tolt	21B18	26	26N	9E	1900
Skykomish River					
Lake Elizabeth	21B19	33	26N	10E	2900

NAME	NUMBER	SEC.	TWP.	RANGE	ELEV.
Skagit River					
Beaver Creek Trail	21A4	35	39N	12E	2200
Beaver Pass	21A1	9	39N	12E	3680
Brown Top	21A28a	26	40N	12E	6000
Devils Park	20A4	34	38N	16E	5900
Freezeout Creek Trail	20A1	14	40N	14E	3500
Freezeout Meadows New	20A38	8	40N	16E	5000
Granite Creek	21A29	25	36N	16E	3500
Meadows Cabins	20A8	29	36N	14E	1900
New Hozomeen Lake	20A7	19	40N	14E	2800
Thunder Basin	21A30	10	35N	14E	4200
Baker River					
Baker Pass	21A27a	1	37N	7E	4900
Dock Butte	21A11A	8	36N	8E	3800
Easy Pass	21A7A	19	39N	11E	5200
Jasper Pass	21A6A	17	38N	11E	5400
Komo Kulshan	21A17	31	37N	9E	800
Marten Lake	21A9A	23	38N	8E	3600
Mount Blum	21A18a	27	38N	10E	5800
Rocky Creek	21A12A	20	37N	8E	2100
Schreibers Meadow	21A10A	18	37N	8E	3400
S F. Thunder Creek	21A14A	20	36N	9E	2200
Sulphur Creek	21A13	22	37N	8E	1600
Three Mile Creek	21A15	18	36N	9E	1600
Watson Lakes	21A8	25	37N	9E	4500
Nooksack River					
Bald Mountain	21A19a	7	40N	7E	4400
Canyon	21A20A	20	40N	8E	5100
Glacier Creek	21A23	9-10	38N	7E	3700
Panorama New	21A26	17	39N	9E	4300
Panorama Snow Pillow	21A25SP	17	39N	9E	4300
Twin Lakes	21A21a	16	40N	9E	5200
OLYMPIC PENINSULA					
Dungeness River					
Deer Park	23B4	1	28N	5W	5200
Morse Creek					
Cox Valley	23B14	31	29N	6W	4500
Elwha River					
Hurricane	23B3	36	29N	7W	4500
Skokomish River					
Black and White	23B7	17	24N	5W	4200
Black and White Lakes	23B6	16	24N	5W	4700
Four Stream	23B10	1	23N	6W	3000
Home Sweet Home	23B5	28	25N	5W	5200
Sundown Pass	23B8	25	24N	7W	3900
Soleduck River					
Deer Lake	23B1	14	28N	9W	3900

LEGEND

NUMBERING SYSTEM EXAMPLE

21A7	Snow Course Only
21A7a	Aerial Marker Only
21A7A	Snow Course and Aerial Marker
21A7M	Snow Course and Soil Moisture Station
21A7m	Soil Moisture Station
21A7P	Snow Course and Precipitation Storage Gage
21A7p	Precipitation Storage Gage
21A7SP	Snow Pillow

WATER SUPPLY OUTLOOK

State of Washington
March 1, 1977

Snow measurements made in the state of Washington and tributary areas continue to be the record low, as reported last month. The snow cover for the state now stands at 83 percent below normal, which is more than half of the previous record low ever measured. The result of this low snow pack and the low precipitation since the first of September is going to be record or near record low runoff during the forthcoming snow melt season. Water users of all types will feel this lack of runoff in the upcoming months. To make things even worse, the soil mantle beneath what little snow pack we have is very dry and this soil mantle will absorb even more than normal amounts of precipitation, whether in the form of rain or snow, before any runoff will occur. Reservoirs are in reasonably good shape for this time of year. Power reservoirs should fill, but at the expense of normal releases. Irrigation reservoirs, such as the five in the Yakima Basin, will have trouble filling due to the necessity of water releases for irrigation purposes.

SNOW COVER

There has been a slight increase in the amount of snow water on the ground from that which was reported last month, but this amount is so minor that it will not have any effect on the forthcoming snow melt runoff. The better snow packs are to be found in the northern part of the state and in the tributary basins of the Similkameen, Okanogan and Upper Columbia. The poorest are on the Lower Columbia Drainage and the southwest slopes of the Cascades below the Skagit Drainage. All of the snow cover is in poor shape and these comparisons are relatively minor when relating one area to another. The best snow pack in the state is on the Nooksack River, and that is only 44 percent of average. The poorest is in the Cedar River Drainage, where the snow cover is only 4 percent of normal. Snow was measured on the Olympic Peninsula as of March 1, resulting in a 10 percent of average snow cover which is an improvement from that measured last month which was zero.

RESERVOIRS

As stated above, most of the reservoirs have average or above amounts of water in storage. The exceptions are Coeur d'Alene Lake, Conconully, Lake Chelan, Keechelus and Ross. The power reservoirs in this case have been drawn down for the continued production of power during this winter and runoff has been exceptionally low which has hindered the filling of these reservoirs. The irrigation reservoirs are in good shape now, but water users will have to start withdrawing water from these reservoirs to start their irrigation operations and with this withdrawal, it is unlikely that these reservoirs will completely fill with the spring runoff.

PRECIPITATION

Over most of the state, precipitation was greater during February than was measured during December and January, but this amount is still well below normal. Winter precipitation was only 53 percent of normal in the Columbia Drainage in Canada, 37 percent of normal in the Pend Oreille-Spokane Drainage, and 30 percent of normal in eastern Washington. Central Washington was 38 percent of normal, but the northwestern slopes of the Cascades are 50 percent of normal while the southwestern slopes are only 32 percent. During the month of February, rainfall ranged up to 70 percent of normal on the northwestern slopes of the Cascades.

STREAMFLOW

During the month of February, streamflow continued to be much below normal. The main stem of the Columbia at Birchbank was 79 percent of normal and this deteriorated to 50 percent of average at The Dalles. Where water managers are attempting to refill reservoirs, such as in the Yakima Basin, the outflow of the Yakima, as measured at Parker, is only 11 percent. The adjusted flow is more like 38 percent of average. Areas where precipitation was especially low also reported very poor streamflow during the month, such as the Palouse at Hooper, 12 percent and the Walla Walla at Touchet,21 percent. Forecasts of subsequent runoff for the streams in the state of Washington now range from a low of 22 percent of normal for the Yakima River at Parker, during the April-September period, to a high of 71 percent of normal for the Columbia River at Birchbank. Puget Sound Drainages are forecast to be between 40 and 50 percent of normal. The forecast for the Columbia River at The Dalles has been lowered five percent from that previously reported and the outflow is now expected to be 53,000,000 acre feet which is 3,000,000 acre feet less than the previous low of 1926. Numerical forecasts can be found on the following pages.

STREAMFLOW FORECASTS - MARCH 1977

e following summarized runoff forecasts are based principally on mountain snow-ver and on the assumption that precipitation and temperature will be near average om the present time to the end of the forecast period. Appreciable deviations om normal of temperature and/or precipitation will correspondingly modify these recasts. Streamflow figures for 1976 are preliminary and subject to revision.

		Seasonal Streamflow in Thousands of Acre-Feet					
sin, Stream and Station	Forecast Runoff 1977	% 15-Yr. Avg.	Fore-cast period	1976	1975	1974	15-Yr. Average 58-72
		COLUMBIA BASIN					
LUMBIA RIVER SYSTEM							
lumbia River	33000	71	Apr-Sept	53937	41101	54411	46410
at Birchbank 1/	25000	67	Apr-July	38979	32944	44439	37548
	17800	65	Apr-June	26054	22429	31853	27549
lumbia River	40200	58	Apr-Sept	80974	66501	88368	69020
at Grand Coulee 1/	32200	55	Apr-July	62715	55870	75997	58368
	24400	53	Apr-June	46556	41377	58725	46049
lumbia River	43600	58	Apr-Sept	86849	73553	96238	75290
bl.Rock Island Dam 1/	35000	54	Apr-July	67890	62727	83339	64181
	26300	52	Apr-June	50520	46759	64205	50594
lumbia River	53000	51	Apr-Sept	122876	108901	139431	104600
at The Dalles, Or 1/	41000	45	Apr-July	99965	94195	123171	89875
	31500	43	Apr-June	79164	73012	98926	73143
ND OREILLE RIVER SYSTEM							
nd Oreille River	7200	45	Apr-Sept	17638	16946	21551	15950
l.Box Canyon	6600	45	Apr-July	15979	15271	20103	14677
	6100	48	Apr-June	13687	11814	16732	12767
TTLE RIVER SYSTEM							
ttle River	1130	60	Apr-Sept		1860	2831	1873
nr. Laurier	1080	60	Apr-July		1779	2752	1794
	950	58	Apr-June		1592	2476	1640

Observed flow corrected for storage in any of the following reservoirs which are above the station: Kootenay Lake, Hungry Horse, Flathead Lake, Pend Oreille Lake, F. D. Roosevelt Lake, Lake Chelan, Coeur d'Alene Lake, Brownlee, Noxon Reservoir and pumpage at F. D. Roosevelt Lake.

Basin, Stream and Station	Forecast Runoff 1977	% 15-Yr. Avg.	Fore-cast period	1976	1975	1974	15-Yr Averag 58-72
		Seasonal Streamflow in Thousands of Acre-Feet					
KETTLE RIVER SYSTEM (Cont.)							
Colville River	59	40	Apr-Sept		225	286	148
at Kettle Falls	52	38	Apr-July		203	269	137
	46	36	Apr-June		187	252	128
SPOKANE RIVER SYSTEM*							
Spokane River	915	31	Apr-Sept	3215	3418	4801	2982
at Post Falls, ID 2/	900	31	Apr-July	3069	3275	4682	2899
	855	31	Apr-June	2884	3033	4409	2773
OKANOGAN RIVER SYSTEM							
Similkameen River	610	40	Apr-Sept	1967	1434	2216	1516
nr. Nighthawk	560	39	Apr-July	1743	1339	2092	1424
	510	42	Apr-June	1357	1092	1710	1222
Okanogan River	690	40	Apr-Sept	2135	1582	2757	1723
nr. Tonasket	610	38	Apr-July	1785	1437	2534	1582
	520	38	Apr-June	1361	1181	2029	1349
METHOW RIVER SYSTEM							
Methow River	410	40	Apr-Sept		992	1665	1031
nr. Pateros	355	37	Apr-July		911	1555	963
	290	35	Apr-June		728	1268	832
CHELAN RIVER SYSTEM							
Chelan River	625	50	Apr-Sept	1467	1364	1749	1253
at Chelan 3/	575	52	Apr-July	1189	1210	1508	1112
	440	54	Apr-June	829	858	1115	881
Stehekin River	490	54	Apr-Sept		1040	1223	904
at Stehekin	415	53	Apr-July		796	996	776
	355	59	Apr-June		526	717	600
Entiat	100	42	Apr-Sept		268	387	239
nr. Ardenvoir	92	42	Apr-July		244	347	220
	80	45	Apr-June		182	256	180

* Forecasts made by Jack A. Wilson, Soil Conservation Service, Boise, Idaho.
2/ Observed flow corrected for storage in Coeur d'Alene Lake and diversions by Spokane Valley Farms Company and Rathdrum Prairie Canals.
3/ Observed flow corrected for storage in Lake Chelan.

ısin, Stream and Station	Forecast Runoff 1977	Seasonal Streamflow in Thousands of Acre-Feet: % 15-Yr. Avg.	Fore-cast period	1976	1975	1974	15-Yr Average 58-72
ENATCHEE RIVER SYSTEM							
enatchee River at Plain	670	51	Apr-Sept		1396	1910	1312
	610	52	Apr-July		1262	1652	1187
	445	46	Apr-June		924	1188	956
enatchee River at Peshastin	860	45	Apr-Sept	2134	1920	2556	1786
	795	48	Apr-July	1795	1738	2232	1629
	615	46	Apr-June	1261	1279	1632	1324
temilt Basin nr. Wenatchee	55	40	Apr-Sept	144*	134*	141*	138*
AKIMA RIVER SYSTEM							
akima River nr. Martin 4/	64	45	Apr-Sept	153	168	231	142
	57	43	Apr-July	140	154	214	131
	50	44	Apr-June	116	127	170	116
akima River at Cle Elum 5/	405	42	Apr-Sept		1112	1463	968
	380	43	Apr-July		1012	1335	877
	322	42	Apr-June		852	1067	764
akima River nr. Parker 6/	380	22	Apr-Sept		2229	3216	1730
	365	21	Apr-July		2141	3092	1701
	320	20	Apr-June		1859	2601	1580
achess River nr. Easton 7/	52	42	Apr-Sept	131	154	207	125
	50	43	Apr-July	119	145	193	118
	43	41	Apr-June	97	120	156	106
le Elum River nr. Roslyn 8/	235	49	Apr-Sept	560	539	745	477
	220	50	Apr-July	483	492	664	437
	185	49	Apr-June	366	388	500	372
umping River nr. Nile 9/	57	39	Apr-Sept	174	179	230	146
	49	37	Apr-July	150	163	206	134
	43	38	Apr-June	108	119	152	112

Thousands of Miners' inches.
/ Observed flow corrected for storage in Lake Keechelus.
/ Observed flow corrected for storage in Keechelus, Kachess and Cle Elum Lakes and diversion by Kittitas Canal.
/ Observed flow corrected for storage in Keechelus, Kachess, Cle Elum, Bumping and Rimrock Lakes and diversions by Roza, Union Gap, New Reservation, Old Reservation and Sunnyside Canals.
/ Observed flow corrected for storage in Lake Kachess.
/ Observed flow corrected for storage in Lake Cle Elum.
/ Observed flow corrected for storage in Bumping Lake.

Basin, Stream and Station	Forecast Runoff 1977	Seasonal Streamflow in Thousands of Acre-Feet % 15-Yr. Avg.	Fore-cast period	1976	1975	1974	15-Y Avera 58-7
YAKIMA RIVER SYSTEM (Cont.)							
American River							
nr. Nile	47	37	Apr-Sept		149	203	128
	41	35	Apr-July		137	181	118
	36	33	Apr-June		104	137	110
Tieton River	96	39	Apr-Sept	308	299	402	247
at Tieton Dam 10/	82	39	Apr-July	245	253	334	211
	67	39	Apr-June	180	187	253	172
Naches River	285	32	Apr-Sept		1054	1428	889
nr. Naches 11/	265	33	Apr-July		952	1286	810
	225	33	Apr-June		761	1038	698
Ahtanum Creek	14	29	Apr-Sept		57	83	48
nr. Tampico 12/	12	27	Apr-July		51	76	44
	11	28	Apr-June		44	64	39
LOWER COLUMBIA RIVER SYSTEM							
Mill Creek	13	48	Apr-Sept		39	57	27
nr. Walla Walla	10	42	Apr-July		34	51	24
	8	38	Apr-June		30	47	21
Lewis River	630	47	Apr-Sept	1333	969	1952	1341
at Ariel 13/	605	53	Apr-July	1161	1022	1760	1151
	530	52	Apr-June	1012	885	1489	1028
Cowlitz River	1070	51	Apr-Sept		2127	3323	2101
Bl. Mayfield Dam	890	48	Apr-July		1852	2976	1846
	870	55	Apr-June		1451	2416	1578
Cowlitz River	1550	56	Apr-Sept	3030	2646	4128	2773
at Castle Rock 14/	1330	55	Apr-July	2550	2278	3694	2416
	1250	60	Apr-June	2115	1816	3029	2083

10/ Observed flow corrected for storage in Rimrock Lake.
11/ Observed flow corrected for storage in Bumping and Rimrock Lakes and diversions by Tieton, Selah Valley, Wapatox Canals and City of Yakima.
12/ Observed flow of North and South Forks (Combined).
13/ Observed flow corrected for storage in Lake Merwin, Yale and Swift Reservoirs.
14/ Observed flow corrected for storage in Mayfield Reservoir.

asin, Stream and Station	Forecast Runoff 1977	Seasonal Streamflow in Thousands of Acre-Feet					
		% 15-Yr. Avg.	Fore-cast period	1976	1975	1974	15-Yr. Average 58-72
	OLYMPIC PENINSULA						
UNGENESS RIVER SYSTEM							
ungeness River nr. Sequim	91	55	Apr-Sept		149	205	165
	75	55	Apr-July		118	162	137
	60	58	Apr-June		82	111	104
	PUGET SOUND						
KAGIT RIVER SYSTEM							
kagit River at Newhalem 15/	1200	50	Mar-Aug		2339	3169	2418
REEN RIVER SYSTEM							
reen River bl. Howard Hansen Dam 16/	180	46	Mar-Sept		418	573	386
EDAR RIVER SYSTEM							
edar River nr. Cedar Falls	47	52	Apr-Sept		101	145	91
LWHA RIVER SYSTEM							
lwha River nr. Port Angeles	235	43	Apr-Sept		544	752	546
	195	43	Apr-July		435	606	456

5/ Observed flow corrected for storage in Diablo, Ross and Gorge Reservoirs.
6/ Observed flow corrected for storage in Howard Hanson Dam.

COMPARISON OF SNOW COVER WITH THAT OF PREVIOUS YEARS

The following tabulation of Washington stream basins presents the water content of the snow about March 1, 1977 as percent of the same date in 1976 and 1975 and average of record.

Tributary Basin	No. of Courses Average	Snow Water Expressed as percent of 1976	1975	1958-72 Avg.
		UPPER COLUMBIA BASIN		
Pend Oreille	14	33	29	32
Kettle	16	44	36	41
Colville	5	24	14	19
Spokane	6	31	28	31
Okanogan	37	34	30	36
Methow	7	15	12	15
Chelan	5	25	24	31
Entiat	11	22	24	28
Wenatchee	9	17	14	20
Yakima	29	29	12	11
Ahtanum	2	12	9	12
		LOWER COLUMBIA		
Mill Creek	3	7	7	9
Klickitat	1	15	9	14
White Salmon	2	9	9	9
Lewis	17	7	8	8
Cowlitz	3	11	11	12
		PUGET SOUND		
White	3	15	11	15
Green	11	9	5	8
Cedar	7	4	2	4
Snoqualmie	4	7	8	8
Skykomish	3	15	14	17
Skagit	14	21	20	24
Baker	5	20	24	25
Nooksack	5	29	30	44
		OLYMPIC PENINSULA		
Elwha	1	7	11	10
Dungeness	1	-	-	9

RESERVOIR STORAGE - 1000 Acre Feet

IN OR EAM	RESERVOIR	USABLE 1/ CAPACITY	Measured (March) 1977	1976	1975	Normal*
		COLUMBIA				
kane	Coeur d'Alene Lake	225.1	17.1	130.0	58.9	162.4
umbia	Franklin D. Roosevelt Lake	5232.0	2937.5	3370.7	4304.9	2843.8
umbia	Banks Lake	714.9	714.9	714.9	706.9	588.3
nogan	Conconully Reservoir	13.0	8.4	10.7	11.2	11.6
nogan	Salmon Lake	10.5	9.5	9.8	9.2	7.4
lan	Lake Chelan	676.1	222.1	463.0	155.1	234.9
		YAKIMA				
ima	Keechelus Lake	157.8	79.8	124.1	95.4	105.5
hess	Kachess Lake	239.0	203.8	204.0	153.6	183.6
Elum	Lake Cle Elum	436.9	408.3	327.0	267.4	264.5
mping	Bumping Lake	33.7	9.2	8.5	2.8	10.2
eton	Rimrock Lake	198.0	129.8	148.0	121.6	128.2
		PUGET SOUND				
agit	Ross Reservoir	1404.1	659.7	1128.6	782.4	873.9
agit	Diablo Reservoir	90.6	86.8	87.5	86.9	85.0
agit	Gorge Reservoir	9.8	8.2	8.2	8.8	-

Based on Active Storage

15-year Average 1958-72

SOIL MOISTURE - MARCH

Drainage Basin and Station	Number	Elev.	Profile Depth	(Inches): Total : Capacity :	Soil Moisture Content (Inches) as of Mar. 1 1977	1976	1975
OKANOGAN							
Salmon Meadows	19A2M	4500	48	5.4	1.9	3.6	2.0
Trout Creek	3-M	3600	48	7.3	3.3	-	3.2
YAKIMA							
Domery Flat	21B20m	2200	48	6.9	-	-	-
Lake Cle Elum	21B14M	2200	48	12.8	-	-	-
WALLA WALLA							
Couse	17C3m	3650	48	11.1	7.5	-	9.3
Helmers	17C2M	4400	48	12.0	9.4	-	10.8
WENATCHEE							
Upper Wheeler	20B7M	4400	48	12.7	6.9	11.4	8.6

FALL SOIL MOISTURE

Drainage Basin and Station	Number	Elev.	Profile Depth	(Inches): Total : Capacity :	Soil Moisture Content (Inches) as of Oct. 1 1976	1975	1974
OKANOGAN							
Salmon Meadows	19A02M	4500	48	5.4	3.4	3.2	1.8
Trout Creek	3-M	3600	48	7.3	3.4	3.1	3.0
YAKIMA							
Domery Flat	21B20m	2200	48	6.9	-	-	-
Lake Cle Elum	21B14M	2200	48	12.8	-	-	-
WALLA WALLA							
Couse	17C3m	3650	48	11.1	-	7.3	-
Helmers	17C2M	4400	48	12.0	-	6.5	-
WENATCHEE							
Upper Wheeler	20B7M	4400	48	12.7	-	8.6	5.4

PRECIPITATION 1/

Division Average Observations and Departures

rainage ivision	FALL Sept-Oct 1976 2/ Observed	FALL Sept-Oct 1976 2/ Departure	WINTER Nov. 1976 - Feb. 1977 2/ Observed	WINTER Nov. 1976 - Feb. 1977 2/ Departure
olumbia in Canada	3.10	- 1.92	7.14	- 6.42
end Oreille - Spokane	1.54	- 2.50	5.62	- 9.40
ortheastern Washington	0.87	- 1.60	2.38	- 5.73
outheastern Washington	1.45	- 1.06	2.69	- 6.08
entral Washington	1.24	- 3.51	8.07	-16.13
orth Central Washington	0.61	- 0.98	2.46	- 3.32
orthwest Slope Cascades	6.65	- 6.56	23.61	-23.49
outhwest Slope Cascades	4.30	- 4.37	11.32	-24.16

ortheastern Washington - Lower Spokane, Colville, Sanpoil and Lower Kettle Drainages.

outheastern Washington - Touchet, Tucannon and Palouse Drainages.

entral Washington - Yakima, Wenatchee and Chelan Drainages.

orthwest Slope Cascades - Puget Sound Drainages.

outhwest Slope Cascades - Lower Columbia Drainages.

/ - Preliminary analysis by National Weather Service from data furnished by Meteorlogical Services of Canada and the National Weather Service.

/ - Departure from 15-year (1958-72) drainage division average.

WASHINGTON SNOW COVER

DRAINAGE AREAS

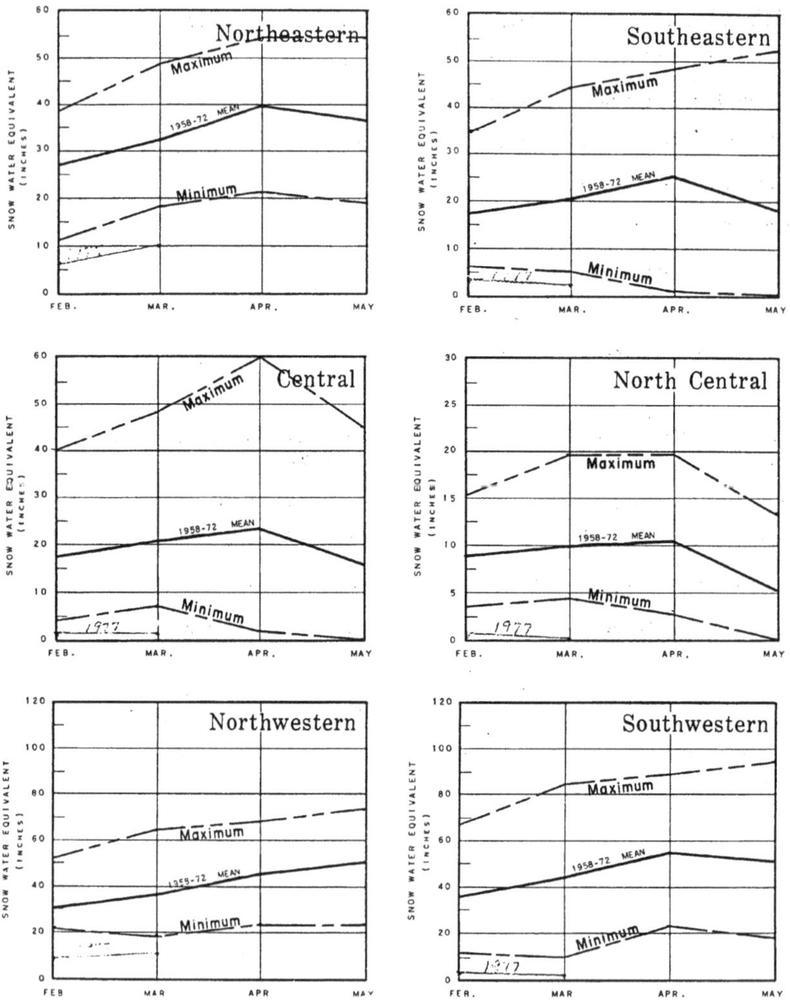

Selected Snow Survey Courses by Soil Conservation Service

WASHINGTON VALLEY PRECIPITATION

1976-1977

DRAINAGE AREAS

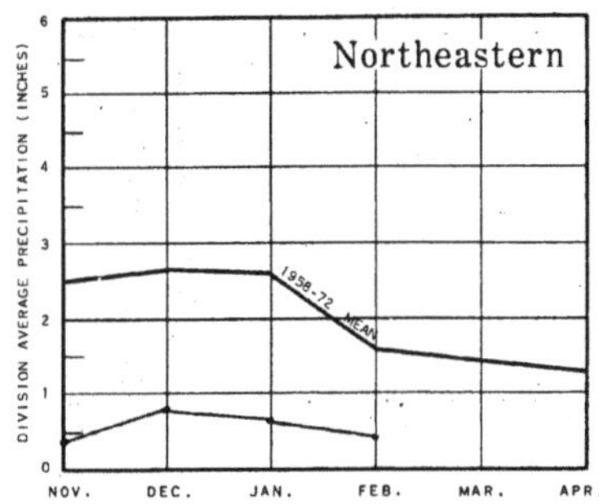

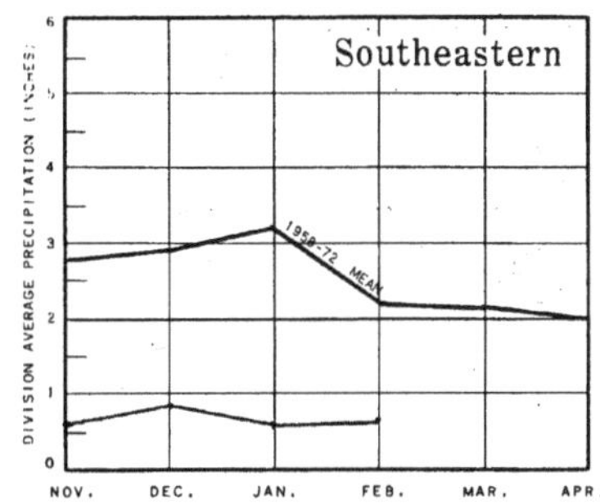

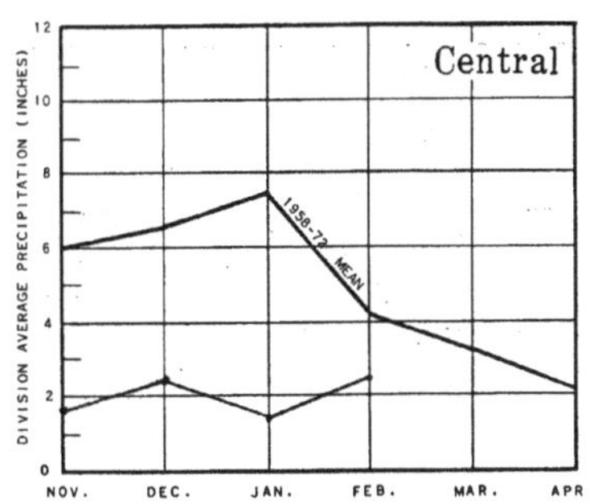

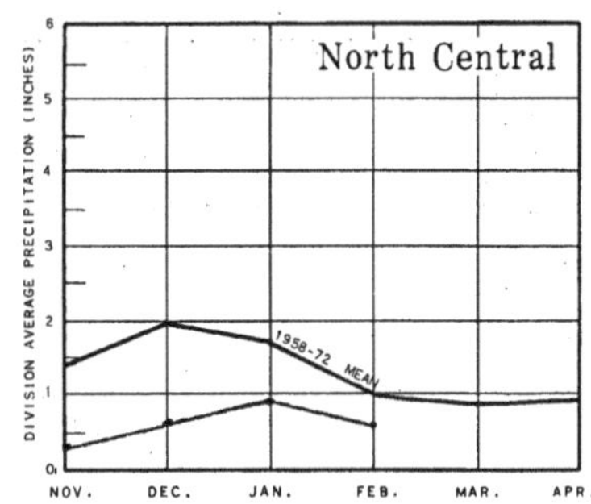

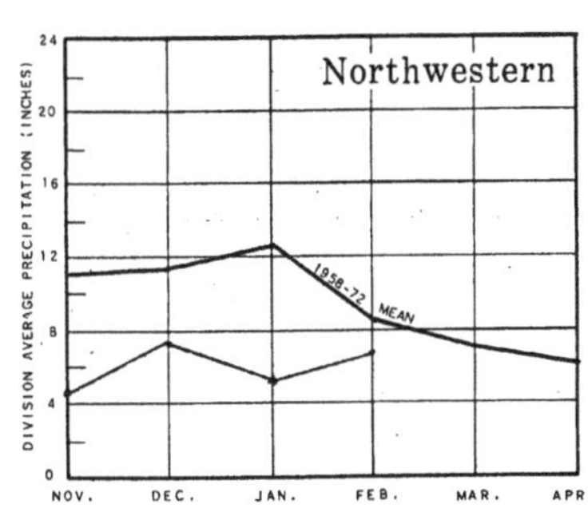

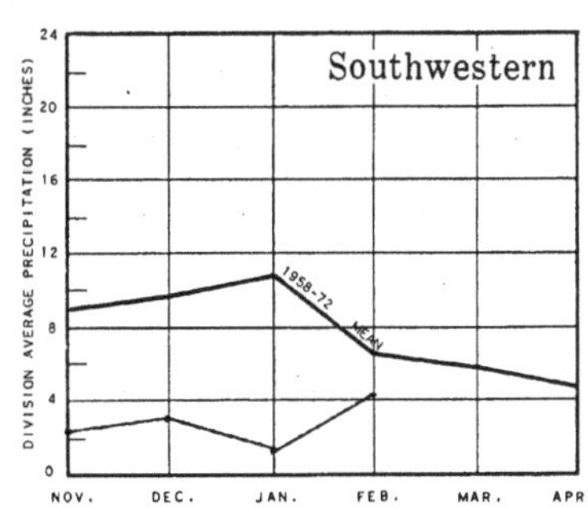

Preliminary Analysis by National Weather Service

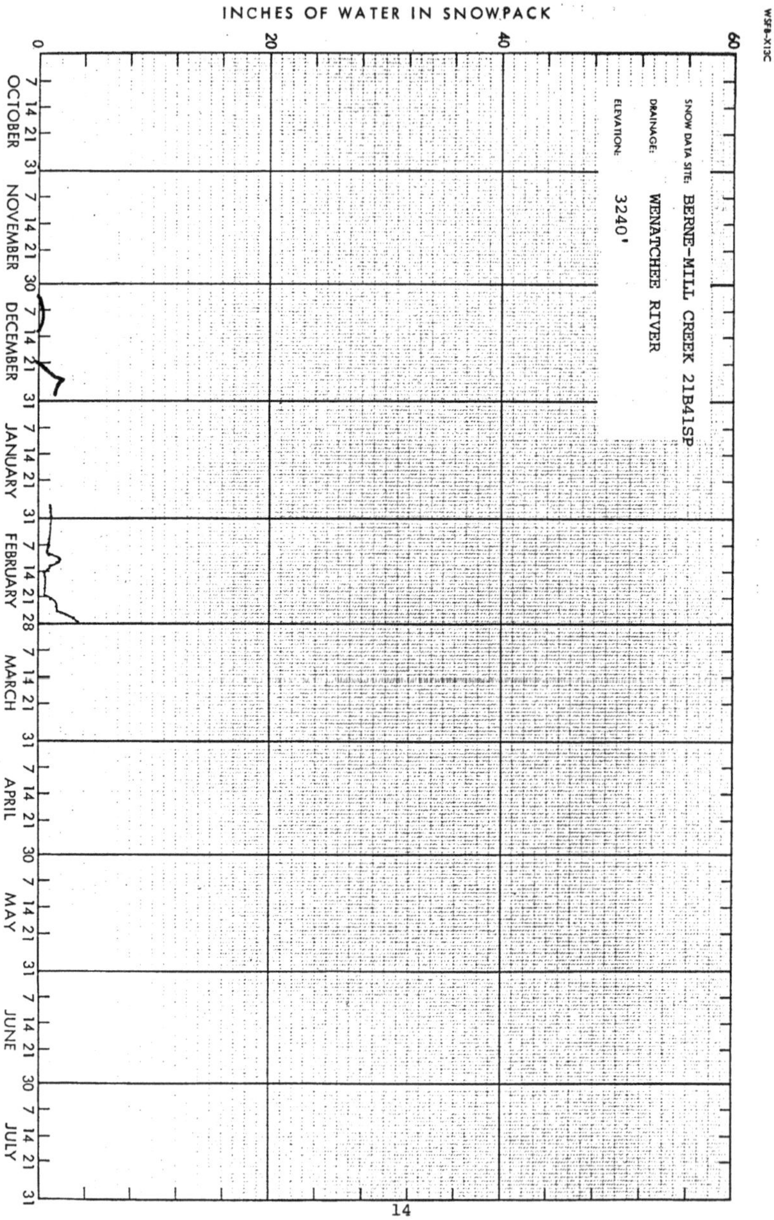
INCHES OF WATER IN SNOWPACK
0
20
40
60
SNOW DATA SITE: BERNE-MILL CREEK 21B41SP
DRAINAGE: WENATCHEE RIVER
ELEVATION: 3240'
OCTOBER
NOVEMBER
DECEMBER
JANUARY
FEBRUARY
MARCH
APRIL
MAY
JUNE
JULY
WSFB-X13C

WSFB-X13C

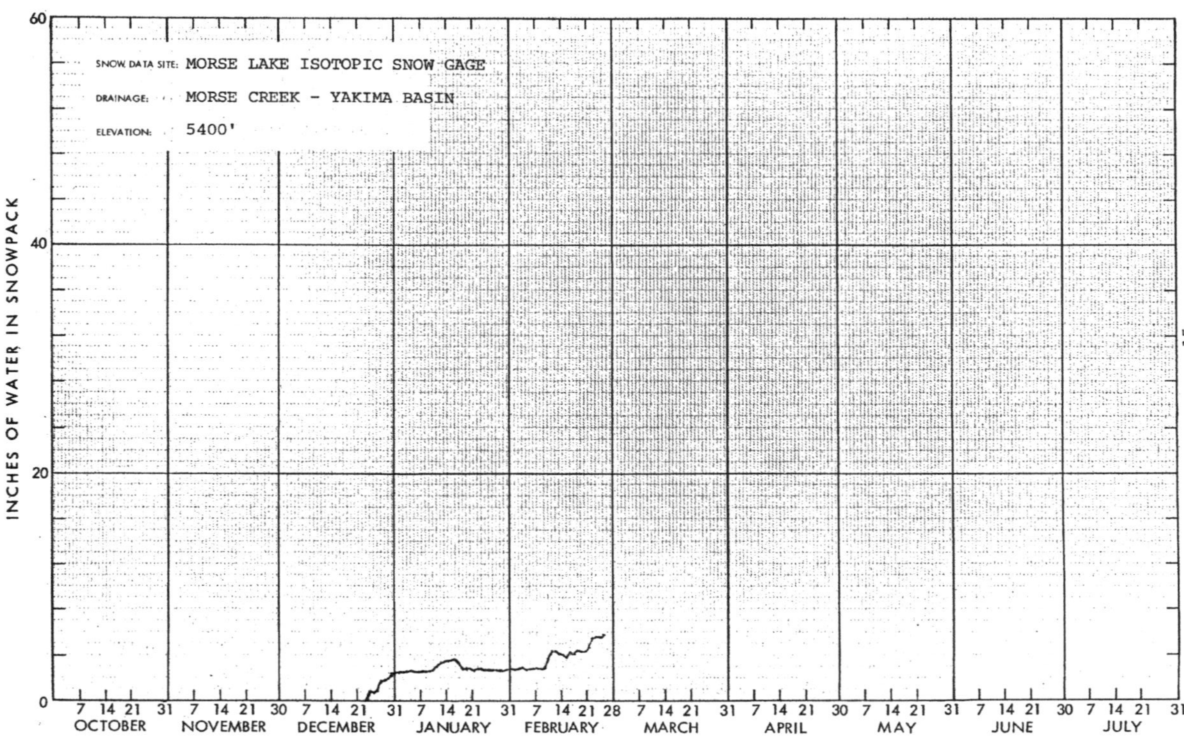
SNOW DATA SITE: MORSE LAKE ISOTOPIC SNOW GAGE
DRAINAGE: MORSE CREEK - YAKIMA BASIN
ELEVATION: 5400'
INCHES OF WATER IN SNOWPACK
0
20
40
60
7 14 21 31 OCTOBER
7 14 21 30 NOVEMBER
7 14 21 31 DECEMBER
7 14 21 31 JANUARY
7 14 21 28 FEBRUARY
7 14 21 31 MARCH
7 14 21 30 APRIL
7 14 21 31 MAY
7 14 21 30 JUNE
7 14 21 31 JULY

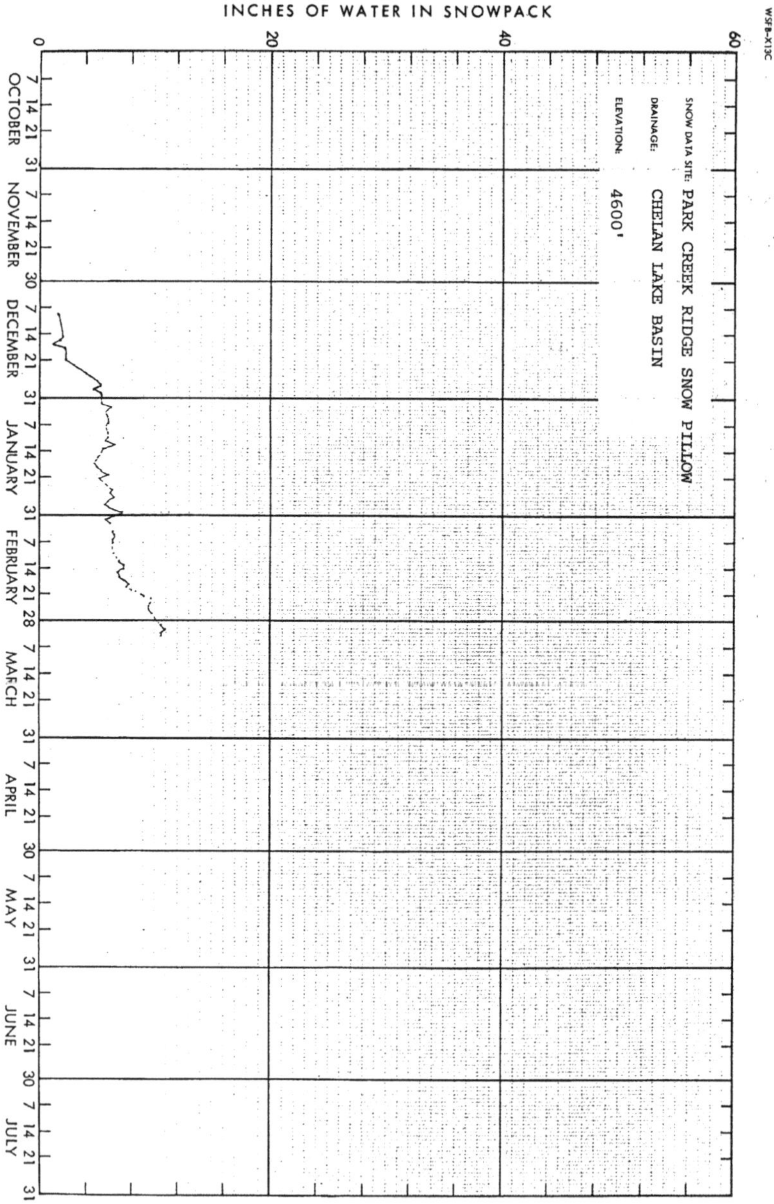
WSFB-X13C
INCHES OF WATER IN SNOWPACK
0
20
40
60
SNOW DATA SITE: PARK CREEK RIDGE SNOW PILLOW
DRAINAGE: CHELAN LAKE BASIN
ELEVATION: 4600'
OCTOBER
NOVEMBER
DECEMBER
JANUARY
FEBRUARY
MARCH
APRIL
MAY
JUNE
JULY

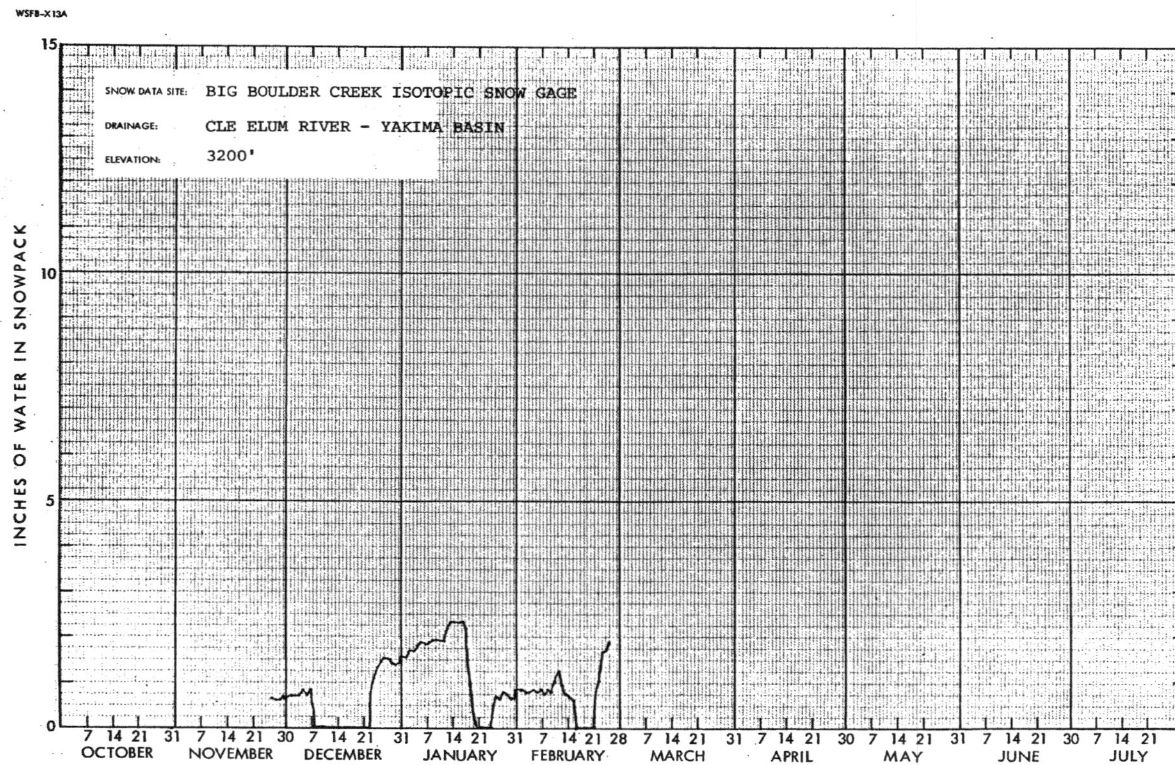
WSFB-X13A
SNOW DATA SITE: BIG BOULDER CREEK ISOTOPIC SNOW GAGE
DRAINAGE: CLE ELUM RIVER - YAKIMA BASIN
ELEVATION: 3200'
INCHES OF WATER IN SNOWPACK
0
5
10
15
7 14 21 31 7 14 21 30 7 14 21 31 7 14 21 31 7 14 21 28 7 14 21 31 7 14 21 30 7 14 21 31 7 14 21 30 7 14 21 31
OCTOBER NOVEMBER DECEMBER JANUARY FEBRUARY MARCH APRIL MAY JUNE JULY

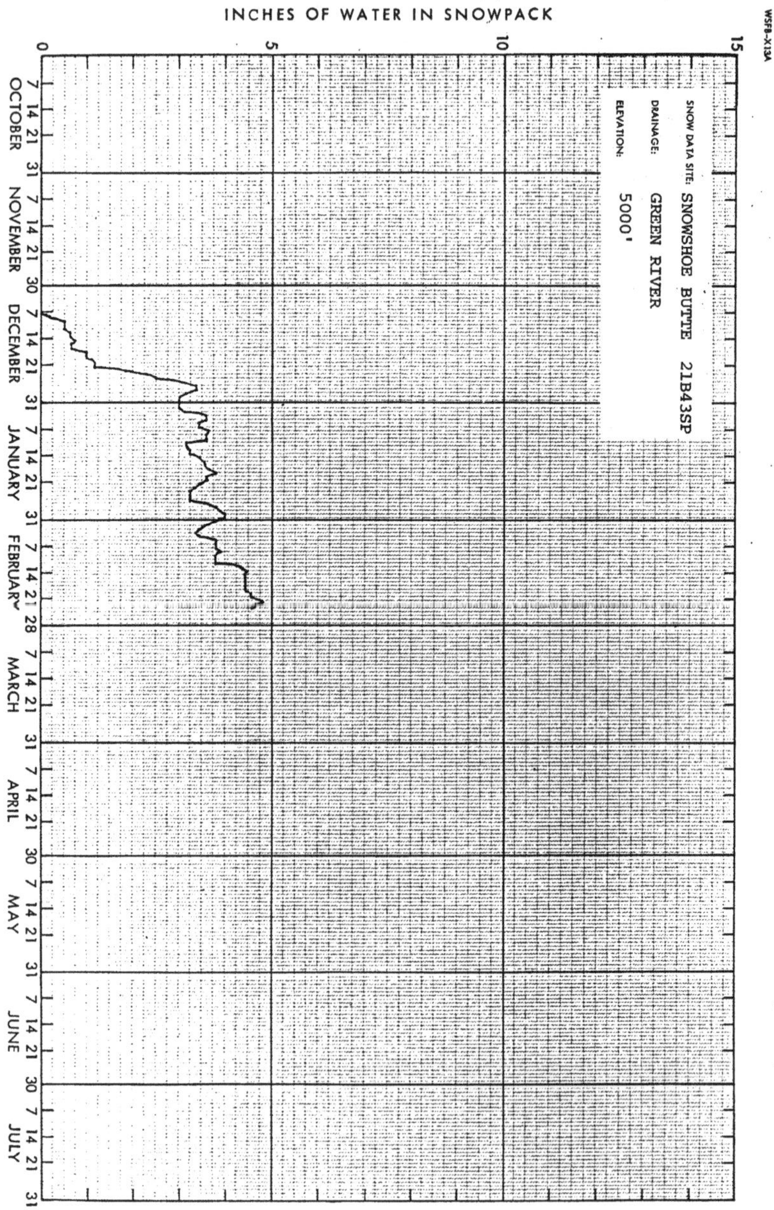
WSFB-X13A
INCHES OF WATER IN SNOWPACK
0
5
10
15
SNOW DATA SITE: SNOWSHOE BUTTE 21B43SP
DRAINAGE: GREEN RIVER
ELEVATION: 5000'
OCTOBER
NOVEMBER
DECEMBER
JANUARY
FEBRUARY
MARCH
APRIL
MAY
JUNE
JULY

WSEB-X4-L

SNOW DATA TO MARCH 1, 1977 - APPENDIX 1

SNOW

DRAINAGE BASIN and/or SNOW COURSE			THIS YEAR			PAST RECORD Water Content (inches)	
NAME	Number	Elevation	Date of Survey	Snow Depth (Inches)	Water Content (Inches)	Last Year	Average #
UPPER COLUMBIA DRAINAGE							
PEND OREILLE RIVER							
Baree Creek	15B11	5500	2/28	56	19.5	53.3	43.6
Baree Midway	15B16	4600	2/28	52	16.5	37.3	34.6
Baree Trail	15B15	3800	2/28	6	1.0	9.4	10.5
Benton Meadow	16A02	2344	2/24	6	1.6	4.6	6.1
Benton Spring	16A03	4900	2/24	16	4.1	11.2	17.4
Boyer Mountain	17A02	5250	2/25	19	4.3	17.8	23.7
Brush Creek Timber	14A13	5000	2/24	14	3.4	8.7	11.7
Chewelah	17A04	4923	2/26	18	3.9	11.6	16.2
Heart Lake Trail	14C10	4800	3/1	30	6.7	22.3	21.2
Hoodoo Basin	15C10	6000	3/1	58	14.8	48.6	46.1
Hoodoo Creek	15C01	5900	3/1	51	12.2	45.5	43.2
Lookout	15B02	5250	2/24	36	10.0	31.2	32.7
Mosquito Ridge	16A04A	5100		Late Report		33.8	34.7
Nelson	19-Can	3050	2/28	24	5.5	12.7	14.7
Schweitzer Bowl	16A06	4500	2/25	29	8.2	20.8	27.8
Schweitzer Ridge	16A05	6100	2/25	36	11.5	40.0	39.9
Winchester Creek	17A03	2970	2/25	8.1	2.0	7.7	12.1
KETTLE RIVER							
Barnes Creek	90-Can	5300	2/24	45	12.5	18.9	18.4*
Big White Mtn.	154-Can	5500	2/26	35	8.4	21.4	18.3*
Boulder Road	18A02	1450	2/28	4.9	0.8	4.6	4.9
Butte Creek	18A03	4070	2/28	17	3.4	7.2	9.3
Cabin Creek	18A08	3170	2/28	16	2.5	6.8	8.2
Carmi	126-Can	4100	2/26	13	2.5	7.0	6.6*
Farron # 1	17-Can	4000	2/28	19	2.9	11.5	12.5*
Farron # 2	243-Can	4000	2/28	19	3.1	10.9	13.9*
Goat Creek	18A04	3595	2/28	12	2.9	5.3	7.1
Graystoke Lake	5-Can	5950	2/28	32	6.9	15.0	19.6*
Monashee Pass	48A-Can	4500	2/24	33	8.8	13.8	12.9*
Snow Caps Creek	18A05	2150	2/28	6.5	1.2	4.4	5.1
Snow Caps Trail	18A06	2720	2/28	8.8	2.5	5.3	6.7
Summit G. S.	18A07	4600	2/28	12	2.5	5.7	7.4
Trapping Creek Lower	166-Can	3050	2/26	8.7	2.3	7.0	5.6*
Trapping Creek Upper	165-Can	4450	2/26	23	5.1	11.6	9.8*
COLVILLE RIVER							
Baird	17A06	3215	2/26	11	2.9	6.1	7.1
Carlson	18A09	2885	2/26	0	0.0	4.9	4.6
Chewelah	17A04	4925	2/26	18	3.9	11.6	16.2
Stranger Mountain	17A05	4990	2/26	10	1.9	8.2	13.1
Togo	18A10	3370	2/26	6	1.2	10.9	10.9

\# Average based on 1958-72 average

* Average for years of record

SNOW DATA TO MARCH 1, 1977 - APPENDIX 2

SNOW

DRAINAGE BASIN and/or SNOW COURSE			THIS YEAR			PAST RECORD	
NAME	Number	Elevation	Date of Survey	Snow Depth (Inches)	Water Content (Inches)	Water Content (inches) Last Year	Average #
SPOKANE RIVER							
Above Burke	15B08	4100	2/24	36	8.8	22.6	-
Copper Ridge	16B02	4800	2/22	29	7.8	25.3	25.7
Forty-nine Meadows	15B03	5000		Late Report		-	-
Granite Peak	15B13A	6000		Late Report		-	37.7
Kellogg Peak	16B05A	5560		Late Report		-	-
Lookout	15B02	5250	2/24	36	10.0	31.2	32.7
Lost Lake	15B14A	6000		Late Report		-	51.3
Lower Sands Creek	16B01	3400	2/22	23	6.2	17.8	17.5
Medicine Ridge	15B04A	6150		Late Report		-	38.5
Mosquito Ridge	16A04A	5110		Late Report		33.8	34.7
Roland Summit	15B05A	5200		Late Report		31.6	31.3
Sherwin	16C01	3200	2/24	13	3.5	15.8	13.8
Sunset	15B09A	5600		Late Report		32.7	33.7
OKANOGAN RIVER							
Aberdeen Lake	6A-Can	4300	2/28	16	3.4	6.9	6.1*
Blackwall Mountain	100-Can	6250	2/24	32	8.5	43.4	33.1*
Bouleau Creek	31-Can	5000	3/1	Not Measured		10.7	11.2*
Bouleau Lake	234-Can	4580	3/1	32	6.5	13.3	14.6*
Brenda Mine	193-Can	4800	2/28	24	5.1	14.5	13.9*
Brookmere	27-Can	3200	2/25	11	2.7	7.3	9.2*
Carrs Landing Upper	168-Can	3200	3/1	Not Measured		5.4	4.8*
Clark +	19A08a	7000	3/1	Not Measured		-	19.7
Enderby	130-Can	6250	2/28	78	21.0	41.0	33.8*
Esperon Creek Lower	164-Can	4400	2/28	20	3.5	11.1	12.0*
Esperon Creek Middle	163-Can	4700	2/28	26	5.2	13.8	15.0*
Esperon Creek Upper	162-Can	5400	2/28	29	6.2	16.5	18.3*
Freezeout Meadows New	20A38	5000	2/23	30	12.4	34.6	25.7
Graystoke Lake	5-Can	5950	2/28	32	6.9	15.0	19.6*
Hamilton Hill	107-Can	4900	2/24	24	4.9	20.0	14.8*
Harts Pass	20A05A	6500	2/23	46	12.3	49.1	38.8
Horseshoe Basin +	19A05a	7000	3/1	Not Measured		-	11.6
Isintok Lake	152-Can	5510	2/27	12	2.0	8.5	8.2*
Lost Horse Mountain	105-Can	6300	2/25	19	2.9	10.4	8.9*
Loup Loup	19A07	4650	2/25	1.8	0.4	5.5	9.5
McCulloch	4-Can	4200	2/28	17	3.5	7.4	6.4*
Missezula Mountain	106-Can	5100	2/25	15	3.0	9.6	9.5*
Mission Creek	5A-Can	6000	2/28	44	10.5	19.1	18.1*
Monashee Pass	48A-Can	4500	2/24	33	8.8	13.8	12.9*
Mount Kobau	156-Can	5950	2/28	15	2.4	9.2	12.5*
Muckamuck +	19A09a	6390	3/1	10	3.0	15.0	15.1
Mutton Creek No. 1	19A01	5700	2/24	0	0.0	7.6	12.9
Mutton Creek No. 2	19A04	6000	2/24	3.2	0.6	9.7	13.3
Mutton Creek No. 2 SP	19A11SP	6000	2/24	-	0.0	6.6	New

\# Average based on 1958-72 average

* Average for years of record

\+ Snow water equivalent estimated from aerial stadia observation

WSFB-X4-L

SNOW DATA TO MARCH 1, 1977 - APPENDIX 3

SNOW

DRAINAGE BASIN and/or SNOW COURSE			THIS YEAR			PAST RECORD Water Content (inches)	
NAME	Number	Elevation	Date of Survey	Snow Depth (Inches)	Water Content (Inches)	Last Year	Average #
OKANOGAN RIVER (Cont.)							
New Copper Mountain	46A-Can	4300	2/28	5.5	1.2	4.9	6.1*
New Penticton Res. #2	183-Can	5225	2/28	19	3.7	9.1	8.6*
Nickel Plate Mtn.	47-Can	6200	2/26	20	4.7	9.4	7.3*
Oyama Lake	203-Can	4400	3/1	Not Measured		-	7.1*
Paysayten +	20A28a	4300	3/1	23	6.9	20.2	15.4
Postill Lake	55-Can	4500	2/28	24	4.9	8.2	7.6*
Quartette Lake	3A-Can	4000	2/28	9.8	2.0	18.8	10.9
Rusty Creek	19A03	4000	2/24	0	0.0	3.9	7.1
Salmon Meadows	19A02	4500	2/24	0	0.0	6.1	9.9
Silver Star Mountain	99-Can	6050	2/27	54	14.3	31.5	24.9*
Starvation Mtn. +	19A10a	6750	3/1	20	6.0	16.2	18.3
Summerland Reservoir	3A-Can	4200	2/26	18	3.8	10.2	9.3*
Touts Coulee	19A06	2845	2/24	1.5	0.3	2.9	4.0
Trout Creek	3-Can	4700	2/25	17	2.7	8.6	6.7*
Vaseux Creek	233-Can	4600	2/28	16	2.6	5.9	7.9*
White Rocks Mountain	70-Can	6000	2/25	26	7.1	22.9	20.1*
METHOW RIVER							
Billy Goat Pass +	20A10a	6409	3/1	Not Measured		28.8	25.8
Dollar Watch +	20A29a	7000	3/1	Not Measured		27.3	25.8
Harts Pass	20A05A	6500	2/23	46	12.3	49.1	38.8
Horseshoe Basin +	19A05a	7000	3/1	Not Measured		-	11.6
Loup Loup	19A07	4650	2/25	1.8	0.4	5.5	9.5
Mutton Creek No. 1	19A01	5700	2/24	0	0.0	7.6	12.9
Mutton Creek No. 2	19A04	6000	2/24	3.2	0.6	9.7	13.3
Mutton Creek No. 2 SP	19A11SP	6000	2/24	-	0.0	6.6	New
Rusty Creek	19A03	4000	2/24	0	0.0	3.9	7.1
Salmon Meadows	19A02	4500	2/24	0	0.0	6.1	9.9
War Creek Pass +	20A31a	6500	3/1	Not Measured		-	40.5
CHELAN LAKE BASIN							
Cloudy Pass +	20A22a	6500	3/2	40	11.2	45.3	37.4
Greenwood Flat +	20A25a	3540	3/1	Not Measured		-	22.9
Little Meadows +	20A24a	5275	3/2	40	11.2	46.8	39.9
Lyman Lake	20A23A	5900	3/2	70	19.7	64.5	52.5
Park Creek Flat +	20A13a	2220	3/1	Not Measured		-	31.4
Park Creek Ridge	20A12A	4600	3/2	39	11.0	55.2	41.9
Petersons +	20A16a	3730	3/1	35	10.5	41.8	32.9
Rainy Pass	20A09	4780	2/24	44	12.3	45.4	36.0
Safety Harbor	20A30A	6300	3/1	Not Measured		30.6	25.7
War Creek Pass +	20A31a	6500	3/1	Not Measured		-	40.5

Average based on 1958-72 average
+ Snow water equivalent estimated from aerial stadia observation.
* Average for years of record

WSFB-X4-L

SNOW DATA TO MARCH 1, 1977 - APPENDIX 4

SNOW

DRAINAGE BASIN and/or SNOW COURSE NAME	Number	Elevation	THIS YEAR Date of Survey	Snow Depth (Inches)	Water Content (Inches)	PAST RECORD Water Content (inches) Last Year	Average#
ENTIAT RIVER							
Blue Creek G. S.	20B28a	5425	2/23	42	13.4	39.5	New
Brief	20B19	1600	2/26	0	0.0	9.4	7.5
Entiat Meadows +	20A33a	4540	2/23	46	14.7	-	45.7
Entiat River Trail +	20A34a	3325	2/23	28	10.6	26.4	21.8
Four Mile Ridge +	20B27a	6800	2/23	12	3.8	43.4	-
Fox Camp +	20A36a	6510	2/23	60	19.2	60.5	54.6
Pope Ridge	20B20	3540	2/24	5.6	2.1	18.2	16.5
Pugh Ridge +	20A32a	6725	2/23	23	7.4	37.2	34.5
Shady Pass	20A37	6200	2/25	14	4.4	34.2	-
Snow Brushy +	20A35a	3910	2/23	33	12.5	35.7	37.7
Tommy Creek +	20B21a	4900	2/23	10	3.2	29.0	28.3
WENATCHEE RIVER							
Berne-Mill Creek	21B23	2925	2/14	6.3	2.8	21.2	23.9
			2/28	22	4.5	26.8	24.7
Berne-Mill Creek New SP	21B41SP	3240	2/28	17	2.9	21.8	21.0
Blewett Pass No. 2	20B02	4270	3/1	14	1.9	13.9	14.9
Chiwaukum G. S.	20B16	1810	2/14	5.4	2.7	8.7	11.2
			2/28	7.4	2.9	13.1	11.6
Fish Lake	21B04	3371	2/25	32	7.1	-	31.3
Lake Wenatchee	20B05	1970	2/14	8	3.2	13.6	13.6
			2/28	11	3.7	17.9	13.9
Leavenworth R. S.	20B17	1127	2/15	0	0.0	2.6	5.7
			2/25	0	0.0	3.6	4.2
Lyman Lake	20A23A	5900	3/2	70	19.7	64.5	52.5
Merritt	20B18	2140	2/14	7.8	2.5	12.6	15.5
			2/28	10	2.8	16.4	15.2
Stevens Pass	21B01	4070	2/14	18	6.8	43.3	42.5
			2/28	46	11.7	54.8	45.7
Stevens Pass Sand Shed	21B45	3700	2/14	5.6	2.6	29.0	-
			2/28	24	4.4	37.0	-
SQUILCHUCK CREEK							
Beehive Springs	20B03	4400	2/24	0	0.0	3.1	7.9
Scout-A-Vista	20B04	3400	2/24	0	0.0	5.8	8.1
STEMILT CREEK							
Jump-Off	20B08	4450	2/25	0	0.0	5.6	8.3
Stemilt Slide	20B06	5000	2/25	0	0.0	11.4	15.1
Upper Wheeler	20B07	4400	2/25	0	0.0	5.4	10.1

Average based on 1958-72 average

\+ Snow water equivalent estimated from aerial stadia observation.

USDA SCS PORTLAND OREGON 1973

WSFB-X4-L

SNOW DATA TO MARCH 1, 1977 - APPENDIX 5

SNOW

DRAINAGE BASIN and/or SNOW COURSE NAME	Number	Elevation	Date of Survey	THIS YEAR Snow Depth (Inches)	Water Content (Inches)	PAST RECORD Water Content (inches) Last Year	Average #
COLOCKUM CREEK							
Colockum Creek Upper	20B22	5300	2/25	0	0.0	3.8	-
Colockum Creek Lower	20B23	4300	2/25	0	0.0	5.0	-
Trough # 2	20B25SP	5310	2/25	0	0.0	7.0	New
YAKIMA RIVER							
Ahtanum R. S.	21C11	3100	2/24	1.2	0.5	3.4	6.7
Big Boulder Creek	21B09	3200	2/25	12	2.0	18.0	18.5
Blewett Pass No. 2	20B02	4270	3/1	14	1.9	13.9	14.9
Bumping Lake	21C08	3450	2/15	0	0.0	9.1	15.2
			2/28	0	0.0	15.9	15.3
Bumping Lake New	21C36	3400	2/15	0	0.0	13.5	19.6
			2/28	5.0	1.0	20.3	20.0
Cayuse Pass	21C06	5300	2/23	36	11.4	76.2	70.4
Colockum Pass	20B09	5370	2/25	0	0.0	13.6	14.5
Cooke Creek	20B10	4123	2/25	0	0.0	2.1	6.1
Corral Pass	21B13	6000	2/24	14	3.9	-	34.3
Fish Lake	21B04	3371	2/25	32	7.1	-	31.3
Green Lake	21C10	6000	2/24	12	3.8	33.3	29.1
Grouse Camp	20B11	5385	2/28	12	1.2	13.4	15.3
High Creek	20B12	2930	2/25	0	0.0	6.9	5.2
Joe Lake +	21B46a	4624	2/24	60	18.0	63.0	-
Lake Cle Elum	21B14M	2200	2/15	0	0.0	9.2	8.2
			2/28	4	0.9	13.4	8.1
Lemah Creek +	21B47a	3327	2/24	24	6.0	39.5	-
Manashtash	20C01	3935	2/24	0	0.0	3.2	4.3
Morse Lake	21C17	5400	2/25	24	7.7	47.4	47.7
Nanum	20B13	3875	2/28	3	0.3	8.8	9.6
Olallie Meadows	21B02	3625	2/25	17	3.8	68.3	40.6
Satus Pass	20D01	4030	2/28	3.5	1.2	7.8	8.7
Stampede Pass SP	21B10	3860	2/15	-	4.0	-	34.2
			3/1	-	5.8	37.4	36.2
Trail Creek	20B14	3360	2/25	0	0.0	2.4	2.2
Tunnel Avenue	21B08	2450	2/15	0	0.0	16.0	20.1
			2/26	10	1.2	22.7	21.2
Van Epps Pass +	20B26a	5925	2/24	52	14.6	42.6	-
Walters Flat	20B15	3360	2/28	0	0.0	7.1	6.9
Waptus Lake +	21B49a	3024	2/24	32	8.0	39.5	-
White Pass (E. Side)	21C28	4500	2/15	0	0.0	17.1	20.8
			2/28	8.4	1.4	24.4	22.0
AHTANUM CREEK							
Ahtanum R. S.	21C11	3100	2/24	1.2	0.5	3.4	6.7
Green Lake	21C10	6000	2/24	12	3.8	33.3	29.1

Average based on 1958-72 average

\+ Snow water equivalent estimated from aerial stadia observation.

WSFB-X4-L

SNOW DATA TO MARCH 1, 1977 - APPENDIX 6

SNOW

DRAINAGE BASIN and/or SNOW COURSE NAME	Number	Elevation	THIS YEAR Date of Survey	THIS YEAR Snow Depth (Inches)	THIS YEAR Water Content (Inches)	PAST RECORD Water Content (inches) Last Year	PAST RECORD Water Content (inches) Average #
LOWER COLUMBIA DRAINAGE							
ASOTIN CREEK							
Spruce Springs	17C04	5700	2/25	12	2.0	25.1	23.6
MILL CREEK							
Homestead	17C01	4030	2/23	0	0.0	8.3	7.4
Martin Springs	17C02	4400	2/23	5.1	0.5	12.1	11.9
Tollgate	18D3M	5070	2/25	16	3.1	29.8	21.1
KLICKITAT RIVER							
Satus Pass	20D01	4030	2/28	3.5	1.2	7.8	8.7
WHITE SALMON RIVER							
Cultus Creek	21C12	4000	2/23	22	4.4	43.4	40.5
Surprise Lakes	21C13A	4250	2/23	19	3.2	45.3	44.2
WIND RIVER							
Old Man Pass	21D19	3100	2/23	7.9	0.8	20.1	17.2
LEWIS RIVER							
Blue Lake +	21C22a	4800	2/23	42	10.5	75.0	69.7
Bob's Trail	21C21	2200	2/23	0	0.0	19.8	14.2
Calamity Ridge +	22D01a	2500	2/23	1.0	0.1	8.8	6.7
Council Pass +	21C18a	4200	2/23	18	3.1	48.6	37.1
Cultus Creek	21C12	4000	2/23	22	4.4	43.4	40.5
Divide Meadow +	21C29a	5600	2/23	22	5.5	54.4	50.9
Grand Meadow	21C25	3500	2/23	9.8	1.1	27.5	23.8
Lone Pine Shelter	21C26	3800	2/23	13	2.3	39.0	35.0
Marble Mountain +	22C05a	3200	2/23	10	1.1	32.0	31.4
New Muddy River	22C06	2000	2/23	0	0.0	13.1	10.6
Old Man Pass	21D19	3100	2/23	7.9	0.8	20.1	17.2
Plains of Abraham +	22C01a	4400	2/23	23	4.6	54.4	58.5
Smith Creek Road	22C04	2100	2/23	0	0.0	15.3	17.2
Spencer Meadow +	21C20a	3400	2/23	10	1.1	28.8	21.5
Surprise Lakes	21C13A	4250	2/23	19	3.2	45.3	44.2
Table Mountain +	21C24a	4200	2/23	20	3.6	50.6	41.7
Timbered Peak +	21D18a	3000	2/23	8.0	0.8	22.3	16.0

\# Average based on 1958-72 average
\+ Snow water equivalent estimated from aerial stadia observation.

WSFB-X4-L

SNOW DATA TO MARCH 1, 1977 - APPENDIX 7

SNOW

DRAINAGE BASIN and/or SNOW COURSE NAME	Number	Elevation	THIS YEAR Date of Survey	THIS YEAR Snow Depth (Inches)	THIS YEAR Water Content (Inches)	PAST RECORD Water Content (inches) Last Year	PAST RECORD Water Content (inches) Average#
COWLITZ RIVER							
Cayuse Pass	21C06	5300	2/23	36	11.4	76.2	70.4
Plains of Abraham +	20C01a	4400	2/23	23	4.6	54.4	58.5
White Pass (E. Side)	21C28	4500	2/15	0	0.0	17.1	20.8
			2/28	8.4	1.4	24.4	22.0
PUGET SOUND DRAINAGE							
WHITE RIVER							
Cayuse Pass	21C06	5300	2/23	36	11.4	76.2	70.4
Corral Pass	21B13	6000	2/24	14	3.9	-	34.3
Morse Lake	21C17	5400	2/25	24	7.7	47.4	47.7
GREEN RIVER							
Airstrip	21B24	1800	2/23	0	0.0	6.6	4.4
Charley Creek	21B25	1200	2/23	0	0.0	0.0	1.2
Cougar Mountain SP	21B42SP	3200	2/22	0	0.0	17.6	-
Grass Mtn. No. 2	21B27	2900	2/23	0	0.0	6.8	19.4
Grass Mtn. No. 3	21B28	2100	2/23	0	0.0	1.7	5.7
Lester Creek	21B29	3100	2/23	3.7	1.9	22.2	21.3
Lynn Lake	21B50	4000	2/23	1.2	0.3	7.4	-
Sawmill Ridge	21B31	4700	2/23	10	3.7	36.6	34.1
Snowshoe Butte SP	21B43SP	5000	2/23	18	5.6	46.7	-
Stampede Pass SP	21B10	3860	2/15	-	4.0	-	34.2
			3/1	-	5.8	37.4	36.2
Twin Camp	21B30	4100	2/23	2.5	0.3	19.7	21.6
CEDAR RIVER							
City Cabin	21B03	2390	1/27	0	0.0	-	-
			2/28	4	0.9	17.9	13.5
Mt. Gardner	21B21	3300	1/27	0	0.0	-	-
			2/28	2	0.4	16.2	15.6
Mt. Lindsay	21B16	2500	1/27	0	0.0	-	-
			3/1	5	0.6	10.8	12.8
Mt. Washington New	21B15	3000	1/27	0	0.0	-	-
			3/1	4	0.5	9.8	-
Rex River	21B17	2400	1/27	0	0.0	-	-
			2/28	2	0.6	17.6	8.9
S. F. Cedar	21B06	3000	1/27	0	0.0	-	-
			2/24	2	0.3	17.0	17.3
Tinkham Creek	21B20	3400	1/27	0	0.0	-	-
			2/24	4	0.8	20.5	20.0

Average based on 1958-72 average
+ Snow water equivalent estimated from aerial stadia observation.

SNOW DATA TO MARCH 1, 1977 - APPENDIX 8

SNOW

DRAINAGE BASIN and/or SNOW COURSE NAME	Number	Elevation	THIS YEAR Date of Survey	Snow Depth (Inches)	Water Content (Inches)	PAST RECORD Water Content (inches) Last Year	Average #
SNOQUALMIE RIVER							
Alpine Meadow	21B48	3500	1/27	0	0.0	-	-
			2/28	21	4.1	40.4	-
Lake Elizabeth	21B19	2900	1/27	0	0.0	-	-
			2/25	17	2.6	35.7	36.4
Olallie Meadows	21B02	3625	2/25	17	3.8	68.3	40.6
S. F. Tolt	21B18	1900	2/28	0	0.0	3.6	2.7
SKYKOMISH RIVER							
Lake Elizabeth	21B19	2900	1/27	0	0.0	-	-
			2/25	17	2.6	35.7	36.4
Stevens Pass	21B01	4070	2/14	18	6.8	43.3	42.5
			2/28	46	11.7	54.8	45.7
Stevens Pass S. Shed	21B45	3700	2/14	5.6	2.6	29.0	-
			2/28	24	4.4	37.0	-
SKAGIT RIVER							
Beaver Creek Trail	21A04	2200	2/23	0	0.0	-	13.0
Beaver Pass	21A01	3680	2/23	5.6	1.2	-	28.3
Brown Top +	21A28a	6000	2/23	53	16.0	78.5	-
Cloudy Pass +	20A22a	6500	3/2	40	11.2	45.3	37.4
Devils Park	20A04A	5900	2/23	47	12.6	53.9	39.4
Freezeout Cr. Trail	20A01	3500	2/23	1.9	0.6	14.2	11.8
Freezeout Meadows New	20A38	5000	2/23	30	12.4	34.3	25.7
Granite Creek	21A29	3500	2/24	18	4.7	22.0	-
Harts Pass	20A05A	6500	2/23	46	12.3	49.1	38.8
Klesilkwa	35B-Can	3700	2/23	1.2	0.1	-	13.3*
Lyman Lake +	20A23A	5900	3/2	70	19.7	64.5	52.5
Meadow Cabins	20A08	1900	2/23	0	0.0	11.5	6.8
New Hozomeen Lake	21A30	2800	2/23	0	0.0	15.0	-
New Tashme	26A-Can	2500	2/27	7.5	1.5	14.3	11.6*
Quartette Lake	34-Can	4000	2/28	9.8	2.0	18.8	10.9*
Rainy Pass	20A09	4780	2/24	44	12.3	45.4	36.0
Thunder Basin	20A07	4200	2/23	16	4.2	19.9	19.8
BAKER RIVER							
Baker Pass +	21A27a	4900		Late	Report	93.0	-
Dock Butte	21A11A	3800		Late	Report	78.0	61.3
Easy Pass	21A07A	5200	2/24	65	18.8	79.0	72.0
Jasper Pass	21A06A	5400	2/24	73	23.0	106.0	82.8
Komo Kulshan	21A17	800		Late	Report		
Marten Lake	21A09A	3600	2/24	60	17.5	92.0	67.6
Mount Blum +	21A18a	5800		Late	Report	65.0	58.2
Panorama New	21A26	4300	2/16	20	9.5	48.5	-
			2/27	48	14.0	67.3	-

Average based on 1958-72 average.
* Average for years of record
+ Snow water equivalent estimated from aerial stadia observation.

SNOW DATA TO MARCH 1, 1977 - APPENDIX 9

SNOW

DRAINAGE BASIN and/or SNOW COURSE			THIS YEAR			PAST RECORD Water Content (inches)	
NAME	Number	Elevation	Date of Survey	Snow Depth (Inches)	Water Content (Inches)	Last Year	Average #
BAKER RIVER (Cont.)							
Rocky Creek	21A12A	2100		Late Report		48.0	25.4
Schreibers Meadow	21A10A	3400	2/24	30	10.0	64.0	53.8
S. F. Thunder Creek	21A14A	2200		Late Report		20.0	8.1
Sulphur Creek	21A13	1600		Late Report		-	9.4
Three Mile Creek	21A15	1600		Late Report		-	0.7
Watson Lakes	21A08A	4500		Late Report		-	57.6
NOOKSACK RIVER							
Bald Mountain +	21A19a	4400	2/28	62	18.6	57.4	42.9
Canyon +	21A20a	5100	2/28	97	29.1	81.6	48.3
Glacier Creek	21A23	3700	2/28	14	1.6	-	21.6
Panorama New	21A26	4300	2/16	20	9.5	48.5	-
			2/27	48	14.0	67.3	-
Twin Lakes +	21A21a	5200	2/28	91	27.3	96.2	62.3
OLYMPIC PENINSULA							
DUNGENESS RIVER							
Deer Park	23B04	5200	2/25	8.6	1.7	-	19.6
MORSE CREEK							
Cox Valley	23B14	4500	2/27	31	6.3	44.6	-
ELWHA RIVER							
Hurricane	23B03	4500	2/25	15	2.0	27.9	20.0

\# Average based on 1958-72 average
\+ Snow water equivalent estimated from aerial stadia observation.

USDA SCS PORTLAND OREGON 1973

Agencies Assisting with Snow Surveys

GOVERNMENT AGENCIES

Canada:

Department of Lands, Forests and Water Resources,
Water Resources Service, British Columbia

States:

Washington State Department of Ecology
Washington State Department of Natural Resources

Federal:

Department of the Army
Corps of Engineers
U. S. Department of Agriculture
Forest Service
U. S. Department of Commerce
NOAA, National Weather Service
U. S. Department of the Interior
Bonneville Power Administration
Bureau of Reclamation
Geological Survey
National Park Service

PUBLIC AND PRIVATE UTILITIES

Chelan County P.U.D.
Pacific Power and Light Company
Puget Sound Power and Light Company
Washington Water Power Company

OTHER PUBLIC AGENCIES

Okanogan Irrigation District
Wenatchee Heights Irrigation District

MUNICIPALITIES

City of Tacoma
City of Seattle

Other organizations and individuals furnish valuable information for snow survey reports. Their cooperation is gratefully acknowledged.

Lightning Source UK Ltd.
Milton Keynes UK
UKHW041118290119
336364UK00009B/1764/P

9 780365 239819